I0605903

It can be easy for Christian women to feel like they need to put on masks and perform. Dominique does a wonderful job guiding the believer from untruths to powerful, life-changing truth! Countering the lies we're told is one of the biggest issues in women's ministries today. This book is a must-read for anyone who struggles with their identity and value in Jesus Christ.

FAITH WOMACK, author of *No More Boring Bible Study* and Bible study content creator at Bible Nerd Ministries

God, Where Are You? is a lifeline for anyone tired of pretending everything's fine. Dominique writes with honesty and grace, inviting you to take off the mask, face the hard questions, and experience God's presence—even in the middle of your pain. She doesn't hand out clichés or quick fixes but points you to real hope and truth. If you've ever felt unseen in your struggle, this book is for you!

JENNIFER PARR, host of the *Winning Women Podcast* and cofounder of Let's Equip

Dominique writes from the trenches, not from theory or polished stories. *God, Where Are You?* offers honesty, hope, and a steady biblical vision of God's presence in life's hardest seasons. Her insight, drawn from real struggles and unwavering faith, guides readers to encounter God even in the valley.

BRITTANY J. TURNER, founder of the Seated Sisterhood

This book is a *must*-read for any woman who has ever felt the ache of divine silence. For over twenty years, we have known Dominique Young to be a woman of profound faith and deep authenticity. In *God, Where Are You?* she has poured out—from the depths of her heart—that very same essence. With incredible grace and biblical wisdom, Dominique walks alongside us through the valleys of doubt, rejection, and confusion, not with easy answers but with the steady, loving presence of a friend who reminds us that we are not alone. She gives us permission to feel our emotions while gently guiding our hearts back to the truth of God's unwavering character. This is a book we will recommend to every woman we know who is navigating life's toughest questions.

PASTORS JOHN AND ROSLYN DAS, senior pastors of Revive Church Charlotte

God, Where Are You? is a gentle embrace and a wake-up call for hard seasons. Dominique Young writes with kindness and courage, offering thought-provoking questions, simple practices, and real hope. She takes your hand and leads you to the God who is nearer to you than your next breath. When the enemy whispers, *You're invisible*, these pages remind you that God is with you—you are not alone. He sees you and you matter. If you keep saying "I'm fine" while internally hanging on by a thread, this book is for you. You will find clarity for your confusion, language for your pain, and the strength to keep going. Read slowly; journal and pray as you go. Let this book guide you toward healing.

PASTOR COURAGE MOLINA, founder of She Knows the Word

In *God, Where Are You?* Dominique Young invites readers into a brave space of honesty about our hurt, rejection, and failure, but she doesn't leave us sitting in our pain. With both tenderness and wisdom, she takes us by the hand and leads us toward healing, offering gentle practices and biblical truths that free us from pretending we're fine. Through powerful personal stories and life-giving insights, Dominique reveals the deeper reality that God is with us even in our darkest moments. This truth changes everything: Light pierces the darkness, hope rises from despair, and love fills the emptiest corners of our souls. Written with clarity and compassion, this book allows readers to see their own stories through the lens of faith, hope, and healing. It is a timely and much-needed guide for anyone longing to experience God's presence in the midst of pain.

CHRISTINA PATTERSON, founder and president of Beloved Women

God, Where Are You? is a refreshing and impactful read from a godly woman who has surrendered her life to Jesus and opened her heart wide to share her story. Dominique invites you to reflect on your own experiences, trace God's hand, remember His mission and promises, and embrace who you are in Him no matter the circumstances. Packed with truth and encouragement, this book speaks to the heart of anyone longing to walk faithfully with God. Wherever you find yourself, *God, Where Are You?* offers wisdom and hope for the road ahead.

JENNIFER ROTH, DMIN, spiritual advisor

For the brokenhearted woman who feels overtaken by wave after wave of struggle, *God, Where Are You?* is more than a book; it's a lifeline. In these pages, Dominique Young writes with the honesty of someone who's lived through deep pain and the grace of someone who has found God right in the middle of it.

This isn't a book of clichés. It's a raw, relatable, and faith-filled journey for anyone who has ever whispered, "God, where are You?" and felt met with silence. With the voice of a trusted friend, Dominique gently walks us through doubt, pain, and the journey back to belief.

I've asked that question before. I've worn the mask and held back tears. Dominique's words reminded me I'm not alone, and neither are you. God hasn't abandoned you. He's been closer than you've realized, even in hidden places.

JACKIE SMITH-BELL, author of the "Abiding Hope" Bible plan and founder of She Remains Ministries

Published in alliance with Tyndale House Publishers

GOD, WHERE ARE YOU?

UNMASKING
Your Pain,
UNCOVERING
His Presence

DOMINIQUE YOUNG

NavPress.com

God, Where Are You? Unmasking Your Pain, Uncovering His Presence

A NavPress resource published in alliance with Tyndale House Publishers

The Team:
David Zimmerman, Publisher; Deborah Sáenz, Acquisitions Editor; Elizabeth Schroll, Copyeditor; Lacie Phillips, Production Assistant; Libby Dykstra, Cover Designer; Brandi Davis, Interior Designer

The author is represented by the literary agency of Embolden Media Group, emboldenmediagroup.com.

ISBN 979-8-89802-021-7

Printed in the United States of America

32 31 30 29 28 27 26
7 6 5 4 3 2 1

To my Lord and Savior, Jesus Christ—

Thank You for never giving up on me, even when I wanted to give up on You. When life was heavy and hope felt distant, You remained faithful. You met me in the silence, carried me through the pain, and taught me how to walk through the hard with You instead of away from You. This book is a testimony of Your love, Your patience, and Your unending grace. I give You all the glory.

To my husband, Steve Young—

Thank you for being a steady presence through the many years I've battled depression and anxiety, even as I was teaching others the Word of God. You have stood beside me with unwavering love, encouraged me when I felt weak, and reminded me of God's promises when I struggled to hold on to them myself. You have truly been an extension of God's love for me. I am forever grateful for you.

CONTENTS

Introduction

I GET IT!

Have you ever walked into church and wondered if anyone could tell you were wearing a mask?

As you leaned in for that infamous church hug (the one that gives the appearance of closeness while ensuring that the two bodies don't actually touch), did you ever wonder if the other person could sense your pain? If you're like me, you may have wished for a super-Christian with all the answers to miraculously find you, strip away your façade, and offer tailored advice. You wished to stop pretending to be happy and finally experience true happiness. I get it.

Pain within the modern church is the elephant in the room. It takes up tons of space and everyone tiptoes around it. As a Christian with "enough faith," you're supposed to be able to move mountains, heal sicknesses, and ward off demons. Depression, anxiety, panic attacks, extended grief, and other struggles—we all seem to think those shouldn't be part of a Christian's life, especially not of one who has life all figured out, right?

I remember being confused by these untruths and drowning in traditions that seemed to stifle rather than uplift. I'd escape to bathrooms to hide my panic attacks, plaster on a big smile to conceal my anxiety, and quietly conclude that I didn't have what it took to be a joyful, at-peace Christian. To mask my weaknesses, I took on works. I led our church's praise and worship team, started Bible study groups, and encouraged others. Meanwhile I was falling apart inside, hoping that something I did would show God I was worthy enough for Him to fix me.

All this striving for worthiness landed me on a hard bed at a mental hospital after a breakdown that threatened the safety of myself and those around me. That's the beginning of my journey to find God in the real struggles of life. I learned to trust God with my maskless self, and He led me down uncharted paths of faith and vulnerability.

As we go down this adventure of discovery, you should probably know who your travel buddy is. When I tell people about myself, I tend to start with the roles most important to me. I am a wife, a mom of four amazing kiddos, and the caregiver of my awesome godson. So yep, there are five children living in our house, along with four chickens clucking around outside.

For years I have wrestled with depression, anxiety, suicidal thoughts, and additional mental health concerns that rear their ugly heads anytime my hormones shift. I know that listing these issues may make some people uncomfortable. You may feel the urge to say, "Don't claim that." But bear with me here; I'm giving you some necessary context. My parents are divorced, and my younger years are sprinkled with beautiful moments and traumatic ones.

I have a bachelor of science in psychology and a master of arts in theology. These degrees prove not that I am smart but that I have been searching for God (theology) amid my mental health woes (psychology) for my entire adult life. I have been in more prayer lines than I can count and cried more tears than I can number. Writing this book was a labor of obedience and love. Obedience to the direction I believe God is leading me and love for you, someone who is searching for God in life's pain and trauma.

On this journey I found out that faith isn't a façade; it's not about donning a mask and pretending to have all the answers. It's about embracing the complexities, the doubts, the questions, and the pain that life can bring . . . while trusting Jesus' truthfulness in the here and now and placing all our hope in His promised return.

As Christians, we often grapple with this tension—the tension between our very real hope and faith in Jesus Christ and the reality of the pain, trauma, and suffering we attempt to hide. We fear that our struggles will expose us as inadequate at best or unfaithful at worst, and we desperately yearn for someone to come along, knock off our masks, and show us the way to authentic happiness and unwavering faith.

This book is for all of us who have felt the weight of that mask, fought to maintain the façade, and hoped for someone to rescue us from our pretense. I want you to know that you're not alone in this struggle and that admitting you're hurting is okay. That's where the healing begins.

We're often told that, as Christians, we should have it all together. We're supposed to be unbreakable, armed with unwavering faith and unyielding joy. But the truth is, having faith doesn't mean you never experience pain, doubt, or fear. Rather, it means you let God guide you on life's journey, and you learn to embrace the inevitable bumps, bruises, and brokenness that occur along the way. Clinging to faith while accepting the journey of life will lead you to a profound realization: God isn't absent during your pain; He's right there with you.

So if you've ever worn an invisible mask and felt like a misfit among the "perfect" Christians, know you're not alone. You're not alone if you've ever hidden in the bathroom to escape a panic attack or put on a brave face while consumed by anxiety. If you've ever felt like you don't have the "right stuff" to be a faithful Christian, I want you to know: *You're not alone*.

In the chapters that follow, we'll navigate the tension between faith and pain. We'll uncover the strength that rises from vulnerability and find authentic answers to the questions that have weighed on our hearts. We'll seek the God who isn't absent in our suffering but is right there with us, offering us hope, healing, and a deeper connection to Himself. Together, we will explore the question that echoes in our souls: *God, where are You?*

You may not know where God is right now in your situation. Your eyes may be so blurred with tears that you would struggle to recognize Him even if someone pointed Him out. I understand what it's like to feel alone, abandoned, and forgotten by God because He doesn't seem to be removing your pain or evaporating your tears. But let's embark on a challenge to look for God, not in the distance, but right here in the darkness. We may find that He was never as far off as we thought.

> I am convinced that neither death nor life, neither angels nor demons, neither the present nor the future, nor any powers, neither height nor depth, nor anything else in all creation, will be able to separate us from the love of God that is in Christ Jesus our Lord.
> ROMANS 8:38-39

Part 1

FINDING YOURSELF

The first part of this book is about finding ourselves. Of course, we want to find God, but first we must be honest about where we are. It's possible amid life's traumas and difficulties that it's not God who we have lost; it's *us*. In this section you will uncover where you may have a disconnect and then reconnect with where you are in your unique life and circumstances, which will also help you see where God is in your life and circumstances.

CHAPTER BREAKDOWN

Let's look at an outline of what we'll cover in part 1.

Chapter 1 • Hide-and-Seek: Facing the Truth About Where You Are. In this chapter we will identify where we are mentally and emotionally. When we attempt to hide from ourselves and from others, we lose ourselves. And when we are lost to ourselves, we can find it challenging to find God even if He is right next to us.

Chapter 2 • The Costume Closet: All the Ways We Cover Up Our True Selves. In this chapter we will identify things that we use to cover ourselves up. The invisible costumes that we find ourselves wearing can cause us to feel disoriented and disconnected. Peeling off the masks and removing the costumes will help us see and be seen more clearly.

Chapter 3 • "911, What's Your Emergency?": It's Okay to Be Found Broken. When we call 911, the first thing we do is explain the emergency. But when an emergency hits in our emotional life, we are often scared to say that we are broken. We don't want to admit our heart is in shambles and we have been shoving the pain down. This chapter is about learning to be okay with being found broken.

Chapter 4 • The Lies We're Told: Learning to Stand on the Truth. We have been told countless lies since we were children. Some may seem small, some may seem big, and many may be lies we think we have forgotten. The truth is these lies burrow their way into our hearts and we begin to live our lives, build our relationships, and view God through a skewed perspective. It's time to uncover the lies we're told.

GOALS OF THIS SECTION

In this section you will learn to

- express where you are mentally, emotionally, and spiritually;
- understand which doctrines or cultural teachings promote hiding;
- identify lies from your past that are affecting your life today; and
- admit the areas of your life where you feel pain, brokenness, and hopelessness.

I do not know everything. I am on this journey alongside you. I pray that my experience of finding God amid debilitating depression, health issues, and suicidal thoughts will help you find Him in your darkest places also. I do not want to pretend that God walked me through these struggles in the time it takes to read one book. Community, therapy, Bible study, and tears (a lot of them!) filled the path. I have no intention of taking the place of your therapist, your local community, or God. I am just here to share: *You are not alone*. Perhaps what God showed me in the darkest of seasons will provide a glimmer of light amid the darkness you may be navigating right now.

1

HIDE-AND-SEEK

Facing the Truth About Where You Are

For most of my life, I have been good at hiding.

As a child, I always won at hide-and-seek. I could find crevices that no one else could, and I could contort my body so that no one could see me. Eventually I got so good at this game that I could hide in plain sight. My friends would walk right by me as I held in laughter, watching them search. As I got older, I continued hiding. I hid my pain behind a smile, and as in my favorite childhood game, I could tuck my feelings away in plain sight. At five years old, I thought hiding was fun. It was as if I had the superpower of invisibility. But as an adult, it was lonely. When I gave my life to Jesus at age eighteen, I thought my newfound faith was my ticket out of hiding. *I will finally break free, feel happy, and enjoy life*, I told myself. Imagine my surprise and dismay when the hiding got worse, along with the depression.

The prosperity gospel permeated every sermon I watched at that time. It was in every book I read and was the primary topic of Sunday's lessons at the church I regularly attended. I learned things like "If you have enough faith, you can heal sickness, remove financial difficulties, fix marriage problems, and even get rid of depression." So I began to wield my "faith" like a magic wand. I did it secretly, though, because I didn't want anyone to know I was depressed. I would do what I was taught, ask God for it (whatever "it" was), and then begin thanking Him as if it had already happened. "God, please heal me of depression," I'd pray, and then add: "Thank You for the healing, God. Thank You for healing me from depression. Thank You for healing me." The next day I woke up still sad and depressed, with my true self still hidden.

Perhaps I prayed wrong. I scoured books and sermons, and I came across someone who shared, "Don't beg and plead with God; He's your Father. *Tell Him* what you want." That sounded a little foreign to me because I didn't live in a household where you could go around "telling your father" things. Respectfully requesting something was one thing but commanding? That was a no-no. Still, I figured, *Hey, it's worth a try.* So instead of saying "please," I submitted my plea more like an order: "God, heal me of depression," and then, of course, proceeded with the "thank you" because I had read that was important. Weeks, months, and years later, I was still depressed, still struggling with extreme sadness and hopelessness.

I had attempted to use my "faith" to get what I wanted, but it wasn't working. I had waited in more prayer lines than I care to admit; I had read the books, taken the courses, and listened to the sermons. Yet here I was, even more hidden than before. In childhood, hide-and-seek was a game to play when I wanted to. As a teenager, hiding behind the mask of a smile felt lonely but seemed worth the cost. Later, as a Christian adult who couldn't seem to muster enough faith to fix herself, hiding felt like the only thing left to do. So I began to hide in plain sight, but unlike in the childhood game, I *wanted* to be found. I wanted God to find me, to rescue me, to save me from this depression I was sinking into. I cried daily, and these words bubbled out of my lips more times than I could count: "God, where are You?" I meant that question, that whisper. I really wanted to know where He was. I could not understand what I was doing wrong. Had I upset God? Did I not have enough faith? Was He hiding from me because of a past sin that I hadn't adequately repented of?

A LIFE-CHANGING JOURNEY

This hopeless, hidden dark place that I found myself in for years was the start of a journey that changed my life forever—that of finding God in pain. And now, I am walking with you on your journey because *I get it.* If you live in a world that says, "Don't say you're depressed, or you're claiming it as your identity," "Don't cry too long because you need to act like you know who your Savior is," or "If you're sick it's your fault because you don't have enough faith," it can be very easy to shrink and hide. It can become easy to plaster on a smile and sashay down the church aisle with the response "Blessed and highly favored" to everyone who asks how you're doing.

But I believe you picked up this book because you're tired of hiding. You've cried those tears wondering where God is, and you genuinely want the answer. So let's go on this journey together. It's not an easy one. But trust me—it *is* worth it.

I wrote this book for you because I get it. Because I walked through my own dark place. Because I cried the same prayer night after night. So I will not judge you or tell you to "pull yourself together and act more like a Christian" in these pages. I also won't insist that the reason you're asking *God, where are You?* is because you don't have enough faith to believe He's with you in your pain. Nor will I suggest that this book should be your one-stop shop for figuring out how to get God to fix all the problems in your life.

This book is a journey; it is an opportunity for us to be honest about where we are in our relationship with God and acknowledge the areas where we have felt abandoned by God. The truth is we don't talk about this enough as believers. When was the last time you sat down and admitted to another believer the ways you've felt neglected, rejected, or abandoned by God? Often we cover our pain with an acceptable response to the situation like "God is in control," "It is well," or "God will get the glory." These catchy phrases are true, but they are not the full story. When we limit ourselves to sharing only the safe or polished parts of our experiences with other believers, we miss the opportunity to process the real pain and honest questions we carry—especially in our darkest moments. We push down our frustration toward God as long as we can until, from the depths of our hearts, a broken cry crackles through: *God, where are You?* In this book, we will not shy away from talking about these very real emotions, and I promise I won't shame you for having them.

This book is also an adventure. One thing I love about adventures is that they take you places you never thought you would go. Like any adventure, this book will lead you to discovery. You will discover God in places you never expected to find Him, including in parts of your past where you never noticed Him before. And you will discover *you*, an experience that may be its own adventure.

This book is also a beginning. I will not promise you that I have all the answers. I am not all-knowing, and I will never claim to be. The truth is I need Jesus every day, *just like you*. I am walking alongside you as you acknowledge pain, struggle, and brokenness and discover God where you least expected to find Him. But this book will not be the end of the journey; it is only the beginning. As we go, we will share from the heart—a place we may find uncomfortable—because that's how healing can happen. I am going to be honest and vulnerable with you, and I encourage you to do the same.

WHERE ARE YOU?

Have you ever tried to find someone else when you couldn't determine where you were? The person may have been telling you their exact location, but because you didn't know yours, you had no point of reference.

When I was a teen I was at a park with friends. I decided to explore the wooded area because I love nature and adventure. A few minutes into my aimless wandering I heard a friend shouting my name. She was trying to get my attention because it was time to load up the car and head home. I yelled back, "Where are you?" She told me exactly where she was—by the bathroom in front of the water fountain. I remembered exactly what that looked like because I had passed it at some point during my wandering. The problem was, I didn't know where I was in relation to that spot, so I didn't know how to get to my friend! Eventually she asked me to describe my surroundings, and she used my description and the sound of my voice to find me and take me to the car. I couldn't find my friend not because *she* was lost but because *I* was.

Similarly, how are we supposed to find God if we are not willing to describe our emotional and mental states authentically? Many Christian doctrines encourage us not to be honest about our experiences out of a misguided fear that acknowledging them will somehow make them truer. Our culture is often caught up in semantics and encourages us not to say things like "I have depression" or "I have cancer" because (we're told) that means we accept our situations and therefore can't do anything to change them. But the Bible reveals quite a different truth.

In Mark 9:17, a father speaks up on behalf of his son: "He is possessed by an evil spirit that won't let him talk," he explains (NLT). In Mark 5:23 a father speaks to Jesus on behalf of his daughter: "My little daughter is dying," he declares (NLT). And the Canaanite woman in Matthew 15:22 cries out to Jesus, saying: "My daughter is demon-possessed and suffering terribly." In each of these instances (and in plenty of others in the Bible), the individual comes to Jesus with a clear understanding of a painful circumstance in their life. They do not try to sound politically correct or avoid naming the source of their heartache lest they somehow "claim" it in the process. On the contrary, each person is painfully honest about the situation causing their distress.

Now it is your turn to be painfully honest. Honest about the roles that you hold, honest about the pain and struggle that is present, and honest about why you are here and why you picked up this book. Shame will jeer, *How can you feel this way or admit you are experiencing this? Aren't you a Christian? What's wrong with you?* I encourage you to ignore that voice. The mask of pretense will claim, *You can't say that you are dealing with this pain or that pain*. It's lying. You may even have a script that you regularly recite to mask your true feelings. Ignore that, too. Together, we will lay aside the weight of shame and the mask of pretense. We will trust that there is room for our honest assessment of exactly where we are emotionally and mentally.

I'd like you to share a little bit about how you're doing right now. You may be looking at this page thinking, *There is no way I will share my feelings with a book*, but please, stay with me here. Take out a journal or notebook and answer the following questions:

- What is your name?
- Which roles in your life are most important to you?
- What pain or trauma do you find yourself wrestling with? (Trust me, writing this down doesn't mean you are "claiming it.")
- Why did you pick up this book?

This may seem like a silly prompt, and you may be tempted to skip it, but being honest about where we are emotionally and mentally helps us begin the journey toward healing. Since the Fall, humans have been determined to hide from God and others. Much like Adam and Eve covered themselves with fig leaves, we often cover ourselves with a big smile, makeup, or a busy lifestyle. We walk around outwardly looking like we have it all together while inwardly we're breaking, and the same question God posed to Adam and Eve in Genesis 3:9, I pose to you today: *Where are you?*

Once you've answered the questions, take a deep breath in through your nose and out through your mouth. Give yourself a pat on the back. We may not have uncovered God's presence just yet, but we have taken one step closer to uncovering where you are, and that is worth celebrating.

You may not be excited about what you wrote down, and that is okay. Liking where you are is not a prerequisite for being truthful about where you are. When a person dials 911 after a car accident, they tell the operator where they are, not because they like their current circumstance but because revealing their location is the first step toward getting the help they need.

You may wonder if you can trust God with your authentic assessment of your present emotional and mental state. You may wonder whether admitting your circumstances out loud will make them worse or cause God to dislike you.

In 1 Kings 19:3-4, we find Elijah on the run for his life. God had just worked through him to complete an amazing miracle, but it also caused the queen, Jezebel, to become very angry with him. Verse 3 states, "Elijah was afraid and ran for his life. When he came to Beersheba in Judah, he left his servant there, while he himself went a day's journey into the wilderness. He came to a broom bush, sat down under it and prayed that he might die. 'I have had enough, Lord,' he said. 'Take my life; I am no better than my ancestors.'" In these few verses, Elijah is honest with God about where his heart and mind are. And if you read on in this chapter, you'll see God meet Elijah where he is with food, drink, and love.

This is an example of God's heart, which is often misunderstood when we attempt to block ourselves and others from honest self-assessment. I am here to loose shackles with truth. Being honest about your mental and emotional health does *not* mean you are declaring that you want to be there forever. Being honest about your mental and emotional health does *not* mean you are claiming this as your identity. Being honest about your thoughts and feelings will *not* cause God to turn away from you. Honesty about your thoughts and feelings is just that, and it is necessary for health and flourishing.

When we visit a doctor, they examine us and ask us questions to assess our current physical health. They may write a prescription tailored to our unique needs. Oftentimes in our respective walks as believers, we want to jump to a prescription without a prior examination. For example, consider Philippians 4:8: "Finally, brothers and sisters, whatever is true, whatever is noble, whatever is right, whatever is pure, whatever is lovely, whatever is admirable—if anything is excellent or praiseworthy—think about such things." Some people read this as a prescription for the spirit, mind, and emotions without knowing *why* the Philippians needed this advice. Paul was aware of their struggle: the difficulty and persecution these believers faced by following Jesus amid a culture steeped in nationalistic idolatry and patriotism. The apostle Paul's advice was not given without first knowing the context and very real struggle of his spiritual protégés.

Being honest about where you are is the first part of your journey, and that honesty may come in waves. You may have been able to answer the questions on page 11 quickly, but as you go through your day, more thoughts and emotions may reveal themselves. That happened to me. Once I allowed one true thought or emotion to surface, more began to emerge. Genuine self-assessment can be overwhelming and lead to tears, and you may need professional help sorting through the years of repressed thoughts and feelings (I did). It may feel like work, but it is work worth doing.

A word of caution: Now is not the time to fix the situation. When we feel the uncomfortable emotions and thoughts that we have been attempting to ignore, we can become very focused on "fixing" the situation to bring ourselves to a more comfortable place. This could lead to making decisions before we are ready or attempting to repress the thoughts and feelings all over again. I encourage you to take out your journal and add the thought or feeling that is making you uneasy to the list. Resist the urge to fix or change the emotion right away; instead, acknowledge and record it as you grow more and more aware of your emotional and mental state.

I told you this would be an adventure. It won't be the final solution but the beginning of a voyage. The question plaguing your heart is *God, where are You?* But the question we will start this journey with is *Where are you?* We are trying to discover where you are emotionally and mentally without trying to mask anything. Within the cry to God is also a cry for yourself. A cry to be seen. A cry to be heard. A cry to be found.

When I was a child, sometimes I would get tired of being good at hiding. I wanted my friends to find me. So I would jump out of my hiding spot and say, "Here I am!" and we would laugh. As I grew up, I forgot that that was an option. I had become so used to hiding that I forgot I could jump out and say, "Here I am!" And the longer I hid emotionally, the less I knew where "here" was. It may take a while to be able to express where you are, and that's okay.

TRACING GOD

In each chapter, we will have a section called Tracing God. We will look at Scripture to see what the Bible teaches us about the topic we just covered. This will be followed by reflection questions. The Bible is a great place to get to know the character of God. The truth is we may not always be able to find God's hand or power the way we want to, but if we begin looking for His character and His heart instead, we will be surprised at where we find it. We will learn how to trace God's heart even in life's most challenging moments.

Scripture

> The man and his wife heard the sound of the LORD God as he was walking in the garden in the cool of the day, and they hid from the LORD God among the trees

> of the garden. But the LORD God called to the man, "Where are you?"
>
> He answered, "I heard you in the garden, and I was afraid because I was naked; so I hid."
>
> **GENESIS 3:8-10**

Devotional

This conversation comes immediately after the first human sin. Although our pain and brokenness are not always a direct result of our personal sins, something happens directly after Adam and Eve sin, an emotion that feels familiar when any type of pain or brokenness enters the chat (or world). This emotion, which can also occur when we are depressed, broken-hearted, or anxious, is shame. Pay attention to what happens when shame enters the picture: Adam and Eve hide. Shame causes us to hide from God.

Now let's look at how God interacts with their hiding. He doesn't say, "Adam and Eve, come find Me." He says, "Where are you?" We know that God is all-knowing. He knew exactly where they were, but did *they* know where they were? Were they able to admit where they were? Well, Adam responds, "I heard You in the garden, and I was afraid because I was naked; so I hid."

While it was a good start, Adam and Eve never fully shared their situation with God. They left out some key details. Where were they really? Adam and Eve were craving more power (which they thought the fruit would provide), they were living in shame, and they had sinned. But Adam and

Eve never said any of that. They never fully shared with God where they were.

This introspection that God calls Adam and Eve to in the Garden of Eden is something we see throughout the Bible and throughout our lives. When we are spiraling in shame, whether because of sin, depression, or sickness that hasn't gone away, we begin to hide from God and one another. If we stay in that shame, we will feel lost, alone, and isolated. Shame is a lonely place, and God calls out to us in that place. But He does not say, "Find Me; get up and search for Me." He first asks, "Where are *you*?" When we are painfully honest with our answer, we break free from shame's grasp, and we can trace the grace, mercy, and love of God that are difficult to see when we're hiding. I know that to be true because of what happened when Jesus walked the earth. In His never-ending grace and mercy toward humanity, Jesus came to earth physically. Some people He met were unwilling to admit that they were broken, sinful, lost, and in need of God's love and compassion. They walked around like they had it all together, attempting to hide their weaknesses and limitations under the mask of power and titles. But other people were painfully honest about their circumstances. They admitted, "I have a demon," or "I have an issue of bleeding," or "I am a man of unclean lips." The same Jesus walked before both groups of people, but one group never truly saw Jesus even though He was right there. They couldn't see Him because they never truly saw themselves.

Oftentimes our search for God starts with a search for ourselves. Asking *Where am I?* is the first step out of hiding.

And as we become more and more painfully honest about our circumstances, we will be surprised to find God was never very far away.

Reflection Questions

This is a book not just for reading but also for reflection. Remember, we're on a journey. We will pause often to contemplate where we've been and where we're going. You may write down answers to the questions and then come back hours or days later to add more clarity and honesty to your response, and that's okay. So let's take some time to reflect.

1. Where are you in your emotional life? How do you think you got there?
2. Where are you in your thought life? How do you think you got there?
3. Where are you with your physical body? How do you think you got there?
4. Where are you in your relationship with God? How do you think you got there?

Prayer

Dear God, I pray for the one reading this book. I thank You for leading them here, and I pray that this journey of discovery sets them free from shame and helps them find hope in Your presence even in their pain. There are so many things I desire for them because I know what it's like to feel trapped in the darkness of shame, brokenness, depression, and pain.

In this very moment, I pray that You give them strength to be painfully honest about where they are, to cry the tears they have been holding in, and to tell the truth about the pain in the secret places of their heart. In Jesus' name, amen!

2

THE COSTUME CLOSET

All the Ways We Cover Up Our True Selves

Did you ever dress up in costumes as a child? I was (and still am) a *big* Disney princess fan, and those princess dresses were my go-to costumes. I would twirl around and pretend that I could talk to animals, had a fairy godmother, and could conquer my fears and achieve my dreams. Different places had different costume closets. A friend's house had a few tattered dresses that her mom wouldn't let her wear out of the house, so we envisioned them as fancy ball gowns. At school, they had fancy costumes, and the blue Cinderella outfit was my favorite. At home, I had an assortment of dresses, some too small and some too big, but they kept me twirling for days. The costume closet was my favorite because you never knew what you would find.

It's funny how we mirror things from our childhood in our adulthood. It's almost as if we attempt to go back to our childhood safe places (those emotional or mental spaces—real or imagined—where we once felt secure, accepted, or protected) as we navigate adult pain. Well, I returned to the costume closet in adulthood; only now, the costumes looked different. I realized that every environment I stepped into had an assortment of costumes I could put on. I learned what happy, popular, and even "I've got it all together" costumes looked like in each environment. But possibly the most intricate costume I found was the church one. As an adult, I put on this costume every Sunday, and as I began to lead and teach, I wore it every day. The church costume is partially about the clothes (pantyhose, a slip, and a dress are a *must* in some spaces), but it's more than just that.

First is the smile. It has to be big enough to suggest you are happy, but not so big someone can guess you're faking it. Next there is the praise. This works a lot like the highway; you flow with the speed of traffic. If it's an energetic, stand-up kind of church, don't sit down because they'll think you don't love Jesus, and if it is a sit-down kind of church, then sit down, but don't cry because your tears will be more visible and people may ask what's wrong. I knew the costumes and their intricacies, and I could float through the crowd, appearing as a joyful, Jesus-loving Christian who had it all together—all while screaming and falling apart inside.

Do you have experience with costumes? You can find them in schools, at church, in your profession, and even at your family reunion. These costumes contain everything we've learned about the expectations of the space we're in.

As a Black woman, I know that Black folks have been

playing in costume closets for generations. We even have a fancy name to describe the process—code-switching—and many attribute their success to it. Code-switching is the ability to put on not just a suit jacket but an entirely new identity as we walk into any space. People from groups with a history of oppression can code-switch well. It's almost as if you can be whoever someone wants you to be, even if doing so is detrimental to yourself.

Have you ever stopped to consider how many invisible costumes you put on each day? Or how those costumes have affected your relationship with God and yourself? The costume closet was a fun place as a child (which is probably why it seemed like a safe place as an adult), but the longer I stayed in costume, the more lost I became. This phenomenon of becoming lost in a character is most vividly demonstrated through a technique known as method acting, where performers fully immerse themselves in their roles, often blurring the line between character and self. Actors such as Heath Ledger, Daniel Day-Lewis, and Christian Bale have openly shared the mental and emotional challenges they faced when they struggled to detach from their characters after filming ended.[1] And much like these actors, we can find ourselves trapped and lost behind the costumes that we wear.

Being trapped in a character does not just affect you; it affects all your relationships. The relationships themselves have not changed, but they are now being viewed through the lens of the character you have put on. Some actors who have found themselves lost in their character have expressed that this changed their relationships with others.[2] Even the way we view our relationship with God when in costume can be vastly different from reality.

This alternative reality that we find ourselves living in when cloaked in invisible costumes can cause us to feel distant and estranged from our actual life—and from the God who loves us. It can also cause us to feel disconnected from ourselves, which makes it nearly impossible to experience connection with anyone else. Trust me, I know! For years I found it very difficult to experience love. I was skeptical of everyone who came across my path, and I no longer felt loving or safe, even around my family. After some reflection work, I realized that I was putting on a costume for work to protect me from the pain of criticism. I had become emotionally distant to present myself as powerful and in control. The problem is that I wore this costume every day at work, and the more I wore it, the more often I forgot to take it off. I became the character I was portraying at work in other environments, and I didn't even realize what was happening.

HOW ARE THESE COSTUMES DESIGNED?

The best costume designers for our favorite movies and TV shows have an amazing eye for detail. They make sure that every part of the costume tells a story. The costume must fit the story's time and plot. If a character is a lawyer in a modern-day law firm, it would be strange to see him wearing swimming trunks in the courtroom. He would likely be dressed in a black suit with a tie and nicely shined shoes. The costume designer has to have an eye not only for style but also for culture, and an understanding of the period.

The same goes for our invisible costume closets. They have been developed through our perspective of culture, expectations, and time.

Let's do a little activity. I will ask four questions to help you think about the costumes you are wearing. Write your answers in a journal, if you are able.

1. Where do you find yourself operating in the most elaborate costume?

You may feel like you are absolutely falling apart, but when you walk into this place or you start acting this role, you put on the invisible costume to look like you have it all together. Is it in church, at home, or when you are in mom mode? Perhaps it's when you are with your husband or walk into your job. This question is not meant to cause you to feel shame; in fact, please kick shame out of the room. This question is to help identify a little bit more about where you are.

Now that you've acknowledged where you find yourself operating in the most elaborate invisible costume, let's move on to the next question.

2. What does this costume consist of?

Does it require a smile, no tears, physical closeness with people, a particular action, maybe even certain clothes? Sometimes we become so used to putting on the costume that we forget the parts it consists of. Take a minute to consider your most elaborate costume. Write down what comes to mind, if you are able. Think about your costume without feeling shame about wearing it.

Now that you have a picture of the parts that make up this costume, take a look at my next question.

3. Why do you believe this costume is necessary?

Again we are not judging our response; we are just being painfully honest so that we can uncover where we are. I will give you an example. As a Black American I have heard people talk about their "interview voice." For years many Black people would change the way they talked to sound a bit more like how they believed White people spoke, and women would fix their hair to resemble a straight, flat-ironed look. In that era, going to an interview with an Afro or braids was unheard of. The question is why many people believed these elements of this costume were necessary. It's because they saw that most people working the jobs they were interviewing for were White, so society seemed to be saying that the closer you are to White, the more successful you would be. Some Black people even went so far as to lighten their skin and make sure the names of their children could pass for White on an application, so instead of Tyrone and Keisha they would opt for David and Brittney in hopes that would give their kids a better chance of at least being called for an interview. Inadvertently or intentionally, society seemed to confirm that the closer you are to White, the better chance you will have of getting a job, so we slipped on the invisible costume in hopes that it would bring us success.

Another example is the church costume. Many of my close friends have expressed that they never feel comfortable sharing their pain with church folks. This is quite ironic since the premise of Christianity is recognizing that we are all broken and need a Savior. So why is the church the place we go to hide our brokenness? What are the elements of this church costume, and why do we put them on? For years there was a church dress code, and this is still the case in many places, where you would not be welcomed if you didn't have a dress outfit and nice shoes. One of the few days we were going to go to church when I was a child, my mom decided we wouldn't because my brother had outgrown all his nice clothes and we didn't currently have the money or time to buy him anything new beforehand. So instead of going in the clothes we had, we just didn't go.

During a church leaders' meeting a deacon shared that if she is feeling sad and low, she will not go to church. She will stay home because she believes being seen sad would destroy her "witness." There are so many elements to the church costume, and if this is one that you put on, then you can probably list different elements of it.

The church costume is one you put on to appear not broken and like you have it all together. And it can easily be linked to a belief that *if Jesus truly saved me, I should have it all together, right? If I truly believe in Jesus, then I should not have all these issues. And if I do have all these issues, what does that say about my relationship with Jesus?* Many times when church folks talk about their pain, they will start with a statement like "I know Jesus is good, and I know He will work it out."

Why is that remark necessary? Because we have learned that the presence of difficulty in our lives seems to communicate the absence of God in our lives. So we hide the pain away in shame, hoping no one will think that our relationship with Christ is deteriorating.

Then there is the costume of good works. Whether you are an avid churchgoer or spend most of your time elsewhere, I am sure you have seen or donned the costume of good works before. You wear this costume when you fill your schedule with altruistic works: feeding the hungry, visiting the sick, participating in every church function, helping anyone who has a need. This costume may look good on the outside, but inside it you are burning out and falling apart. You may think this costume is gaining you friends and applause. It's not about the good works, but rather about the acceptance that you crave.

The costume that is meant to protect us from judgmental glances also does another thing within us: It produces cognitive dissonance. The *Merriam-Webster Dictionary* describes *cognitive dissonance* as "psychological conflict resulting from incongruous beliefs and attitudes held simultaneously."[3] Believing that "true Christians have no brokenness in their lives" and striving to appear put together while feeling broken inside produces tension. We start to wonder whether we are saved and whether Jesus really loves us because the tension between these two ideas—*Christians aren't broken* and *I, a Christian, am broken*—has never been addressed. We just wear the costume every day. As the tension grows, the question becomes: Will we slip further into costume until we no longer recognize or are willing to acknowledge any parts of ourselves that are outside that costume, or do we shed the costume and honestly reveal where we are—mentally, emotionally, physically, and spiritually?

In Mark 2 the Pharisees respond with judgment to Jesus having dinner with tax collectors and known sinners. These religious leaders believed that if you ate dinner with a sinner, it did not just speak about their life but about yours as well. The presence of sinners at your table showed that you were *like them*. Jesus responded: "It is not the healthy who need a doctor, but the sick. I have not come to call the righteous, but sinners" (Mark 2:17). Was Jesus saying that the Pharisees were so healthy and righteous that they did not need Him? No, that was not what He was saying at all. Jesus was pointing out that the costumes the religious leaders were wearing were keeping them from what they were truly seeking. The Pharisees sought to appear well, whole, and put together all while being broken, and because of their inward brokenness, they would not come to Jesus. They had gone so deep into character, they no longer realized (or were willing to publicly admit) that they, too, were sick and needed a Savior. The Pharisees also attempted to appear sinless, pretending their rigid adherence to the law made them righteous. They had worn the "holier than thou" costume so long that they denied their need for a Savior and therefore would not sit and eat at His table, confessing their needs. Ironically, the Pharisees were so wrapped up in the character they developed to keep themselves "safe" that it kept them from Jesus, the One who is truly able to save.

The invisible costumes that we wear in different environments are used to cover what we believe are limitations, brokenness, and insecurities. The costume is designed to project what we believe strength looks like so that when others look at us, we appear strong and in control. These attributes are what we seek to feel safe. It's interesting how many of our human interactions are about seeking safety, purpose, and belonging, and these costumes are our attempts to use our God-given creativity to bring about the very things we seek!

Those three questions alone are enough to really uncover some things. But this last question is a tough one. Remember what we talked about in the last chapter about being painfully honest? Well, this one is heavy on pain (at least it was for me). The question is this.

4. What do you fear may happen if you take the costume off?

It's easy to write off this question and say nothing! There have been many times that I avoided it because I didn't think it pertained to me (and I didn't want to admit that I, a Christian, a Bible teacher, was afraid). But when I began to uncover the fear that encouraged me to hold on to the costumes, it was quite painful, but necessary.

So now let's create a safe place for you to be afraid, a place where you don't have to hide. A place where you don't have to preface every feeling with the statement "I love Jesus." Sis, I know you love Jesus or you wouldn't have picked up this book or made it this far with all my Scripture references and Jesus-girl antics. You can answer the question honestly, painfully honestly: *What do you fear may happen if you take the costume off?*

The truth is that fear keeps our pain hidden and unprocessed. Once we expose the fear, we recognize it's not actually fear at its core—it's pain, usually from trauma.

When I realized that my fear of taking off the invisible costume was really a fear of abandonment, my eyes were opened. I recognized that my fear of abandonment came from unprocessed pain of being rejected by peers and loved ones as a teen and young adult. The fear was the cloak, the fabric the costume was made of, but the pain and trauma underneath were what required the most attention. God is leading us to take off the cloak and come to Him with the pain, come to Him with the trauma, come to Him with the brokenness. He won't run away; He will be with us.

As you think about this question, don't rush through the answer. Sit for a moment and process what was just revealed. I encourage you to breathe through it, and if the revelation of the specific fear has been driving the masks and costumes causes tears to fall down your cheeks, let them fall. Don't wipe the tears away to get to the next sentence of the book. This book can wait. Take your time and breathe.

The costume closet is a protection mechanism. It is not just a game of dress-up; the costumes protect you from a perceived threat. The tricky part about these costumes is that they keep the real you hidden. And masks may cover your face, but they also impair your vision. Depending on how intricate a particular mask is, it can make it hard to see even what is right in front of you.

• • •

It may seem strange that a book titled *God, Where Are You?* starts with the topic of finding ourselves. But the costumes and masks we use in our day-to-day lives can make it difficult to find God even when He is right there. The process of identifying what we have been cloaking ourselves with is imperative on this journey.

TRACING GOD

Scripture

> Fear not, for I am with you;
> be not dismayed, for I am your God;
> I will strengthen you, I will help you,
> I will uphold you with my righteous right hand.
>
> ISAIAH 41:10, ESV

Devotional

I understand how cruel it may seem for me to have you uncover your fears and then hit you with a "fear not" Scripture. You may find yourself trying to wipe away your tears and appear strong to obey the Lord's command. Many of us may even envision God telling us, with a booming voice, to "get it together."

But I encourage you to pause and consider what God is *really* saying here. Is He saying, "Get it together" because you're a Christian? Is He saying, "How dare you be afraid"? Is He looking at the one who is afraid with disdain and disappointment? Or is something else happening here?

Imagine for a moment a child is stuck in a burning building, and you are trying to get them out. They went to the place they perceived as safe, which was in a room that was not currently burning. The hallway that leads to true safety (outside) looked dangerous, so they stayed put in their safe space. You find them and say, "Honey, don't be afraid. I've got you."

You are attempting to reassure the child they can leave the place they thought was safe and trust you to lead them to true safety. You would never expect them to quit crying, and you don't want them to feel shame in that moment. "Do not be afraid" is not a condemnation; it is a reassurance that they can find safety in you.

Similarly, the main point of this Scripture is not to fix your fear. In it, God is reassuring Israel and us that He is with us! We can come out of our makeshift "safe spaces" and find our safety in Him.

So often I used to read every "fear not" Scripture as if God was disappointed in me. And because of that, I didn't run toward God but rather cowered away from Him. I would find that makeshift safe space and cover myself in costumes to appear strong and unafraid. I thought that's what God wanted . . . until I realized that in each of these "fear not" Scriptures, God is calling us to Himself, not commanding us to hide. God is not embarrassed by our fear. God is saying we don't have to stay hidden away under all those costumes and hiding places. We can come to God with all our cares, concerns, and honesty, and God will keep us safe. We don't have to pretend because God wants to give us a safe space in Him.

Reflection Questions

1. What pain is your fear covering up?
2. What past events have caused that pain?
3. Have you ever processed this pain? If so, what did that process look like? If not, what steps can you take to begin processing it?

Prayer

Dear Lord, thank You for being willing to be our safe space when we are afraid. You don't rush us out of our pain but rather provide a safe place for us to process our way through it. You don't condemn us for being afraid but rather call us out of our makeshift "safe spaces" and closer to You. Thank You! In Jesus' name, amen!

3

"911, WHAT'S YOUR EMERGENCY?"

It's Okay to Be Found Broken

Have you ever had to dial 911? Do you remember what the call was like? Typically the operator picks up and says, "911, what's your emergency?" At that time, they expect you to tell them what is wrong. They want to know the extent of the emergency, who it has affected, and where it is taking place. The same goes for a doctor. When you go into a doctor's office, they ask, "What brings you here today?" and they want you to identify any areas of your mind or body that feel unhealthy. And we can't forget about therapy. One of the first questions a therapist asks each time you make your way into their office is "How are you today?" They are not looking for the surfacy answer that you give a stranger walking down the street; they want to understand—deeply—your emotional and mental state.

Any medical person you go to for help will try to figure out which parts of you seem injured, unhealthy, less than whole. But you may hold off from seeking medical help because you don't want to be found "broken." I understand. When I started having panic attacks, I waited months to seek help because I was embarrassed. But one day my mental and emotional health became so bad that my thoughts began to scare me.

I remember driving with no destination in mind, tears streaming down my face. My mental and emotional health were rapidly declining, but I had hidden it from everyone. I didn't want anyone to know how broken I was. I led our church's praise and worship team and was preparing to give my initial sermon, and there I was having a mental breakdown. I was scared of my own mind, ashamed that I couldn't fix it, and angry that God was letting this happen. I had no solution except to drive. Perhaps I could outdrive my thoughts.

Eventually I landed in a hospital, where the doctor asked, "What brings you here today?" I shared the thoughts that I had been afraid to speak. My face was so drenched with tears and my eyelids were so puffy from crying, it was surprising that the doctor could look me in the eyes, but he gave me a concerned look. After what seemed like the fastest evaluation in history, he sent me to a behavioral hospital, transported by ambulance to a place that felt miles away. I remember the shock on my husband's face when he first saw me there. He had no idea that my mental and emotional health were in such a bad place. He was concerned for me, and all this was new for him also.

By this time, I had one son and one on the way, and there I was lying on a hard bed inside a mental hospital. They had taken everything from me—my wedding ring, my bra, my shoelaces, anything I could possibly kill myself with—and put me in a dark, cold room. This was my worst nightmare. Now everyone *knew* I was "broken." I had spent years hiding in the bathroom during panic attacks and being extra cheery to mask my extreme sadness and the terrible thoughts that I wrestled with. I had worn all the costumes, and now here I was, exposed. I remember walking those halls thinking, *I've gotta get out of here.* I wanted to put my mask back on, crawl into my costume for the day, and go back to pretending because that is what seemed safe.

My husband came to visit me every day. His look of love and concern wrecked me, and although I tried to put the mask back on when he came, there really was no point because he knew what was going on now. So I spent most of his visit crying and saying, "I don't belong here. Please take me home." But the reality was that at that moment, I did belong there. I *needed* to expose the shattered state of my heart, mind, and soul. But I didn't want to. This was scary. I didn't want to admit my brokenness.

The thing about calling 911 or reaching out to the medical field for help in any situation is that you have to admit something is wrong. We don't often want to do that. We would much rather God heal us in private than be required to expose our inner turmoil in public. We would much rather appear unbroken than admit we need help. Calling 911 for an urgent physical ailment is something that our culture has accepted. Reaching out to the doctor when your physical health is deteriorating seems to make sense. But what happens when your heart is broken or your soul feels wounded? What happens when your emotions feel fragile and your thoughts scattered? For many people what happens is that you push it down and live like nothing is happening, all while screaming internally for someone, anyone to see you struggling.

We often say we want to be seen. But do we want to be found if "being found" means being seen in our brokenness? Calling 911, crying out to a friend, and even crying out to God can't stop with the cry; it must lead to us explaining what hurts.

BEING FOUND BROKEN

The deepest desires for most humans are to be seen, to be known, and to belong. We want to be seen for who we are, known by those we love, and truly belong. This is true in our relationships with other humans and in our relationship with God. Since you picked up a book titled *God, Where Are You?* I would venture to say that you feel a bit unseen right now.

But—do you really want to be found broken? Do you really want to be found weak? Do you really want to be found in need? If you want to be seen and known, do you want even the weakest, most fragile parts of your heart to be seen and known as well? Because if you are hiding the parts you deem "too broken," you may be pushing away the help and love that you truly desire. Have you ever watched a sick child cry because someone had to take him to the doctor? The child wanted to get healthy but was afraid of the place that would help him get well. Similarly someone who has gone through trauma may want to process their grief and pain so that they can feel free but maybe they are afraid of going to therapy.

Oftentimes we don't want to be found broken for at least one of three reasons:

1. We are scared of what people may think of us when they find out just how broken we are.
2. We are scared of healing because the process may cause more pain.
3. We are scared to let go of the pain because we have become so accustomed to it that it has begun to feel like protection.

The truth is that to be seen, known, and loved for who we are, we must be willing to show our broken parts. We must be willing to reveal both *who* we are and *where* we are. If we don't, then we will continue to feel unknown (because we are constantly hiding), unseen (because we are always pretending to be perky and upbeat), and unloved (because we have deemed part of ourselves unlovable).

But what if today we began naming the broken areas that we have been attempting to cover up? What if we began to say "ouch" when it hurts? Even if you were to name the broken parts in a quiet room and keep the discussion between you, God, and this book, you would be taking a step forward. What if you pretended that you called 911 and the operator said, "What's your emergency?" or went to a clinic and the doctor said, "What brings you in today?"—how would you respond?

Take some time to answer these questions:

- What hopes feel broken right now?
- What dreams feel broken right now?
- What relationships feel broken right now?
- What beliefs feel broken right now?
- What other areas feel broken right now?

Take a deep breath. Don't try to rush to fix things. Don't allow shame to convince you that there is something wrong with you because you are acknowledging what isn't okay in your life. Take a deep breath in and blow it out. Take another deep breath in and blow it out.

- How does this brokenness make you feel?
- What does this brokenness make you think?

REVEAL THE PAIN

I remember the first time I was honest about the broken areas of my heart. I remember the first time I was honest about the broken parts of my relationships. I called out the broken parts out loud in my bedroom. And then I cried, and cried, and cried. I didn't have a solution yet, but I did reveal the pain, and that is an important part on this journey of discovering God and locating ourselves.

Have you ever paid attention to a skilled pediatrician? They don't grab a child and force them to do what they need them to do so that they can quickly give them the medicine or the examination they need. Instead, a skilled pediatrician encourages the child to reveal the pain by asking them to point to where it hurts and then walking them through each step they are about to make before they make it. The doctor does not force the child but rather encourages the child to reveal the pain for themselves because if not, the doctor runs the risk of harming the child by forcefully examining a painful spot. In order for the doctor to conduct the examination in a healthy, less painful way, they partner with us by asking us to reveal the pain and brokenness that we feel. We go to the doctor because we want them to find a solution for our pain, but if we hide the pain from them, our actions betray our desire.

Oftentimes it's our hiddenness—not our brokenness—that causes us to feel distant from God. Often the fact that we don't want our brokenness exposed keeps us from calling for help. We are afraid to be seen broken, so instead of asking for the help we need, we stay silent and hope someone sees us . . . while hiding parts of ourselves.

This book is titled *God, Where Are You?*, but oftentimes we can't see God through our own pain. We don't realize how pain obscures our vision. Understanding where we are with pain is an important first step. Rather than jumping to fix it, sit with it and try to understand it. *What* is hurting, *why* something is hurting, and *how* something is hurting are all essential pieces of information.

If you've had a chance to answer the questions on page 40,

here are a few follow-up questions to help you figure out how your emotional state affects your life. It's kind of like when a child comes to you and says, "My elbow hurts," and you reply, "Can you bend it?" You ask this question because you want to see how it affects their overall function. Consider writing your answers in a journal. And remember: This is not about fixing; this is about discovering.

What hopes feel broken right now?

What events in your life have caused these hopes to feel broken?

How has this brokenness affected the way you show up in your life? (For example, have you stopped writing the book you were working on or praying to God for help in this area?)

What dreams feel broken right now?

What events in your life have caused these dreams to feel broken?

How has this brokenness affected the way you show up in your life? (For example, have you stopped writing your dreams in your journal, or have you stopped trying to learn how to achieve them?)

What relationships feel broken right now?

What events in your life have caused these relationships to feel broken?

How has this brokenness affected the way you show up in this relationship or in others? (For example, have you begun avoiding phone calls, or have you stopped praying for certain individuals in your life?)

What beliefs feel broken right now?

What events in your life have caused these beliefs to feel broken?

How has this brokenness affected the way you show up in your life? (For example, have you stopped praying or have you stepped back from studying the Bible?)

What other areas feel broken right now?

What events in your life have caused these areas to feel broken?

How has this brokenness affected the way you show up in your life? (For example, has it changed the way you connect with others, influenced your confidence, or caused you to withdraw from community?)

After this type of reflection you may want to rush and fix the issue, and if you can't figure out how to fix it, you may get the urge to hide it. I encourage you to do neither right now. Instead, I encourage you to breathe. This is part of the journey we're on together. The path has some bumpy terrain, but the destination is worth the discomfort.

The question "God, where are You?" is a layered one, but

at its core it is based on our feeling unseen, usually because of our pain. In the book of Exodus, Israel would cry out to God because the pain they were going through was so great, and because of their circumstances they felt that God did not see them. They felt alone and forgotten. Oftentimes in this modern day we have been taught to ignore our feelings, not cry out. But when we're not honest about how we're really doing, we not only feel abandoned by God and by those around us, but we also feel abandoned by ourselves.

This journey and these activities help us bring back our ability to see our pain for what it is so that we can see God where He is. If we can't see where we are, God could be right there with us and we wouldn't be able to see Him. Our vision must be adjusted so that we can see. Much of what we wrestle with is not just our external circumstances (although they may be hard). Much of the lingering pain and brokenness is within. Our broken heart may not show up on an X-ray, but it can be felt throughout our entire body. Our scattered thoughts may not be physically discernible, but they affect how we communicate. The fear that grips us as we enter a new relationship may appear invisible, but it pulls us in ways we feel deeply. We must be able to see and understand this invisible terrain so that we can also see where God is in it.

I encourage you to keep going. I remember getting to this part of my journey and wanting to quit. I wondered how drudging up all these hurt feelings was helpful. I felt like I was in more pain than when I started. If that's how you're feeling, trust me—*I get it!* I've walked this road, and in some areas I am still walking it. This process is not a quick fix. I hear the grumbles, but go along with me here. Pain will continue to happen on this side of heaven. We live in a sin-fallen world, and Jesus told us: "In this world you will have trouble. But take heart! I have overcome the world" (John 16:33). We may not be able to make all pain disappear, but we can process it because of Christ. Don't quit, don't get discouraged, and don't race to the finish line. This is a journey, and although it can be a bit painful, you will learn more about yourself, your relationship with God will grow, and you will feel more free as you understand how to process the pain, grief, and brokenness. As we begin to understand that the pain and brokenness we feel is not something to hide away but something to be processed, experienced, and understood, it helps us show up in our lives. Even the hard parts are helpful because they are part of the human experience on earth, and God is in the hard parts too. We'll get to the chapters on discovering where God is in all this soon. For now, just trust me—as we open our eyes to where we are, it will help us see where God is. (Spoiler alert: He's not as far as you may think.)

TRACING GOD

Scripture

> During that long period, the king of Egypt died. The Israelites *groaned* in their slavery and *cried out*, and their cry for help because of their slavery went up to God. God heard their groaning and he remembered his covenant with Abraham, with Isaac and with

> Jacob. So God looked on the Israelites and was concerned about them.
>
> **EXODUS 2:23-25,** EMPHASIS ADDED

Devotional

During the beginning of the book of Exodus we see Israel enduring brutal slavery. This was not due to anything they did wrong. This was not a result of a particular type of sin in their lives. They were just multiplying in number and it made the Egyptian pharaoh afraid, so he imposed oppressive slavery on them. Pharaoh had the Egyptians beat the Israelites and kill their sons, and we can only imagine what else happened to this group of people.

We see in these verses that the Israelites cried out because of their slavery. They groaned because of their slavery. They didn't hide their pain. They didn't pretend that they were fine when they were not (although they may have had to do that at times to endure the slavery)—they cried out and God heard them. The Israelites didn't know immediately that God heard them, but He did.

You may have been taught to shove down your feelings, to pretend they do not exist. Perhaps you have been walking through life trying to look like you have faith, but inside your heart is breaking. Not saying "ouch" when we are hurt causes us to become disconnected from ourselves. And in time we may crave that detachment because we don't want to feel the pain anymore (trust me, I understand). But disconnecting from ourselves doesn't keep us from feeling the pain; it stops us from understanding the pain and from seeing God in it. Disconnecting from ourselves and our current situation causes us to feel as if we are drifting, unseen and unanchored.

Crying out and groaning was a powerful thing that Israel did during their oppression because their groans did not go unheard. Their groans were valuable and important to God: "God heard their groaning . . . and was concerned about them" (Exodus 2:24-25). I am here to say the same to you: Your groans do not go unheard. Your reflections and honesty do not go unheard. The groans, the truth, the vulnerability are all important and valuable to God. He hears, He sees, and He knows. There is no need to hide, no need to fear your own brokenness. We can be honest about what hurts and know that it is not indicating a lack of faith but rather an honest assessment of where we are.

The more honest we are about our own emotional state, the more we will begin to recognize where God is. God hears our groaning, and even if He doesn't end the pain right away, He is close enough to hear our cries. The cries of Israel did not fall on deaf ears (even though it may have felt like it in the moment, in their anguish). On the contrary, God hears, He sees, and He knows. And rather than getting annoyed by the Israelites' tears, God was moved by them. Perhaps we, too, should begin to be honest about where we are and how we feel and trust that God hears us as well. This is a call to stop hiding behind the fig leaf of pretend happiness and instead walk in truth even when it hurts, knowing that God hears and responds with concern and compassion.

Reflection Questions

1. As you were answering the questions throughout this chapter, did you journal about something you have been hiding or avoiding? Did anything surprise you about this experience?
2. How does it feel now that you have started to open up about your pain? (No answer is right or wrong. All feelings are valid.)
3. What are some thoughts or feelings that make you shy away from vulnerability?

Prayer

Dear God, thank You for this journey of reflection and honesty. Thank You that You are not a God who is embarrassed by our pain and brokenness. You're not a God who tells us to "fix our face" when we feel like our heart is in shambles. You allow us to come to You broken. You ask us where we are, and You really want to know the answer. You don't want to hear a list of Christian talking points; You really want to hear us, even when what You hear is groans of pain. Lord, teach us how to be honest before You—honest about our pain and honest about areas that feel broken—and help us see You through this journey. In Jesus' name, amen.

4

THE LIES WE'RE TOLD

Learning to Stand on the Truth

Do you remember the first lie you were told that skewed your self-perception? The lie could have been said explicitly or it could have been implied, but it changed the way you looked at yourself and the world around you.

When I was young, I believed the lie that dark-skinned girls are not as pretty as girls with lighter skin. The lighter the skin and the longer the hair, the prettier the girl, I thought. Now, no one explicitly told me this that I can remember, but the message seemed to be pushed everywhere. The main characters of all my favorite movies were the light-skinned girls, and the darker-skinned girls played the best friend. In my favorite singing groups the lighter-skinned, longer-haired girls were typically the lead singers, and the dark-skinned girls, though equally talented, sang the background vocals.

And at school the boys tended to clamor for the attention of the lighter-skinned girls. As a girl with a chocolate skin tone and shoulder-length hair, I was often told, "You're pretty for a dark-skinned girl." This "compliment" produced a belief that dark-skinned girls were not even on the same scale as lighter-skinned girls and even being "pretty for a dark-skinned girl" would never actually make you pretty because anyone lighter skinned than you would always be prettier, more valuable. And let's face it, most girls were lighter than me. The Asian girls, the Hispanic girls, the White girls . . . most girls in these groups were lighter skinned and had longer hair. And even among the Black girls, many were lighter than me, so no matter how pretty I was, I figured I would always be "pretty for a dark-skinned girl." Which still put me at the bottom of everyone's list.

Believing this lie affected the way I showed up. I attempted to overcompensate by becoming the smartest, or the most hardworking, or the most talented girl. I tried to find other ways to be the best in the room since I was born with what I considered a disadvantage. It took me years into my adulthood to peel back the layers of this lie and realize how deeply it influenced the way I showed up in the world. The truth is that there are many lies we are told in childhood that affect the way we show up today. Yet often we do not realize that the way we are living and behaving is based on a lie.

Typically we find that our most toxic behavior is fueled by a lie, often one that we were told in childhood. As children, our minds were very impressionable because we were new humans. We looked to the adults in our lives to help us make sense of the world. And because we did not have many experiences to compare certain things to, it became easy to take one experience, write an entire narrative around it, and determine *This is how life is.* These little lies, because they have been around so long or because we have accepted them so deeply, can be very difficult to uncover.

UNCOVERING THE LIES

One of the most powerful ways I have found to uncover the lies is starting with the behaviors. It is hard to find a lie because they are usually deeply hidden, but the behaviors they produce are much more visible. Even then it can still be a bit challenging to uncover the lies because some lies produce behaviors that we may deem good but are truly toxic. (We will get to those.) Let's start with the lower-hanging fruit: behaviors we view as toxic.

I was a teacher for ten years, and we used a method of teaching called "I Do, We Do, You Do." Which is basically that the teacher models something (solving a math problem, for example, or whatever the class is learning that day) first, then repeats it with the students, and then the students do it on their own. I am going to use this method to show you how it can help us uncover the lies that are fueling our lives.

Let's start with a behavior I noticed in my life. Whenever I had a disagreement with anyone I was close to, I would shut down emotionally and say I agreed with them (even if I didn't *actually* agree) to end the argument. Why did I do this? Why was this a pattern in my life? Let me take you on the journey of discovering.

The first question I explored was *What was I feeling right before exhibiting this behavior?* Almost every time before I shut down, I was afraid that my loved one would leave me. I was afraid that I would push them away. I was afraid of being alone and in danger.

It was strange that I would feel that way, because this happened with my best friend, my husband, and other people I felt secure with. But when disagreements happened, I found myself shutting down and feeling afraid.

The next question I considered was *When was the first time I remember feeling this type of fear?* I realized that the first time I remember experiencing this type of fear was when I was younger. My parents had an interesting relationship, and whenever something was wrong between them, they would meet with my brother and me about someone leaving. I would hear them arguing loudly, and inevitably we would have a "family meeting" to discuss the possibility of them separating. Eventually this happened so often that I became numb to it (and they finally divorced in my college years), but from when I was in elementary school until I left for college, this was the pattern.

Next I asked myself, *What lie did you believe because of this?* The answer was I believed that arguments lead to separation. I didn't realize that I believed this lie until I was older. This is why I would shut down in every hard conversation. I would cower and begin to agree with everything the other person was saying because I was deeply afraid that if I allowed the argument to get too bad, they would leave me. This response produced so much inner tension because I had so many feelings and thoughts I was not expressing that I felt alone, unseen, and unvalued. I felt abandoned by God and by the people who loved me. And it wasn't because I *was* alone; it was because the lie that I was living under had convinced me that I would be.

Now let's try this "uncovering the lies" exercise together. I will give you a few options of behaviors to consider.

- Do you pretend that things are fine when they are not?
- Do you try to fix everything on your own?
- Do you tend to pack your schedule and say yes to invitations even when you don't have space?
- Do you find yourself shutting down in heated conversations (or perhaps you find yourself more argumentative in these situations)?

Choose a behavior out of the ones I listed, or if none of these behaviors resonate with you, choose one of your own. Answer the following questions, going into as much detail as possible to get a better understanding of what was happening at that time.

- What was I feeling right before exhibiting this behavior?
- When was the first time I remember feeling this way?

- What lie did I believe because of this experience? (This narrative is likely the lie that has been feeding this behavior.)

I encourage you to do this activity as many times as needed to uncover the lies that have been fueling your life.

HOW DO THESE LIES AFFECT OUR DOCTRINE?

You may be wondering what uncovering the lies we've been told has to do with finding where we are or finding where God is. Oftentimes we don't realize how these lies influence the way we see our situation, ourselves, and God. The doctrine that we accept is not always biblical; however, it connects with the lies we may believe. Often how we believe God interacts in our lives has less do with what the Bible says and more to do with the lies that are foundational to how we live our lives.

I used to believe that if an argument with a loved one got too bad, that person would leave me. When I realized this was not true, I asked myself, *What part of this lie have I carried into my relationship with God?* This answer was a bit difficult to uncover because I don't go around getting into arguments with God. But as I sat with the question for a while, I realized I was afraid of what might happen if I made a mistake, or if I misunderstood something about the Scriptures and did something wrong. I was afraid God would leave me.

I would perseverate on things such as finding my purpose because I was scared that if I didn't accomplish it, God wouldn't want me. The fear of abandonment that I was experiencing in my relationships with other humans was infiltrating my relationship with God because of a lie that crept in when I was a child. It is easy for these lies to sneak in when we are young because we have no truth yet to combat them with. And by the time we know the truth to combat the lie, we often don't even realize that the lie is there.

So what do we do?

Remember what I said at the very beginning: This is a journey. There were likely many lies that you believed were true in childhood, and now that you are an adult, you don't realize they are distorting your view. When some type of pain happens, even as you get older, a lie can creep in under the disguise of protection. For example, if you have a bad relationship with someone, you may believe you are unlovable. And that lie could make its way into your relationship with God.

Or say you approach work in a very unhealthy way, taking no breaks and no rest, and then you get a promotion. You may start thinking that if you want anything in life, you have to work yourself as hard as you can and stop resting. But this is a lie that will keep you working at an unhealthy pace.

For better or worse, what we believe influences how we live. Because of this it is important to uncover the lies we're told and process them. With each one, we must ask ourselves, *Where did it come from? What is it attempting to protect me from? Has this lie affected the way I view and relate to God?*

It's important to not rush through this journey of uprooting the lies we're told. We can become like a person who is frustrated with the weeds in the garden and just begins frantically yanking them out. There are a few issues with this approach.

The first is that you could accidentally uproot or damage a healthy plant. The second is that with frenzied weeding we often don't get the root. If you have gardening experience, you know that means the weed will grow back. The same goes for the lies in our lives.

We might be tempted to do this reflection activity as quickly as possible to identify and remove as many lies as we can, but the danger with this approach is that we begin to snatch up truth and throw it out with the lies. For example, in the work scenario previously mentioned, if I realized that the lie was that working at an unhealthy pace earns you a promotion, but then I quickly pulled that lie up without processing, I'd run the risk of also uprooting the truth that hard work is important and then perhaps becoming resentful of all work. This can often happen because of quickly uprooting beliefs without questioning if there is a lie, identifying it, and replacing it with truth from Scripture.

We also run the risk of not pulling up the entire root and allowing some of the lie to remain because we didn't process long enough. With every healing step it is important to sit with and process through what is bubbling to the surface. I remember that I was often in a rush to be "fixed." I would do all the reflection activities and read all the books as fast as I could. I thought that the faster I got through the material, the quicker I would be healed. But processing past pain and misconceptions that were affecting my present relationships was not a onetime fix; it is an intentional process that continues throughout a person's lifetime. If we accept that we are on a journey and not in an Olympic race competing with everyone around us for how quickly we can heal, we will enjoy the journey more.

WHAT IS TRUE?

When we realize that a lie is influencing how we live and how we relate to God, we must move into figuring out what is true.

We know what is *not true*, but what does Scripture say about the particular untruth you were believing? For example, what does Scripture say about rest? About acceptance? About being loved? Whatever the main topic of the lie is, search the Scriptures for what God says on the topic, for the truth that counters the lie.

Begin to envision how you will show up in the world standing on this truth. It's one thing to identify what is true, but altering your perspective to align with this truth is another story. For example, say I know that I need glasses. Actually putting the glasses on and seeing the world through those adjusted lenses requires intention. Improved vision won't simply occur because of knowledge; action is necessary. The same thing happens with truth. It's one thing to know that something is true. It's another thing to intentionally look at your circumstances through that truth. If you have ever gotten glasses, you know it takes a little time for your eyes to adjust to them. And for your eyes to adjust, you have to wear the glasses—even when it's uncomfortable.

Uncovering the lies you're told is ultimately uncovering the fears you hold. The kingdom of darkness runs based on fear, but the Kingdom of God runs based on love. Love seems like a very vulnerable position when we are looking at the world through the lens of fear. Love is what led Jesus to the cross, hanging in what would appear to be the most vulnerable position: arms outstretched, battered, and bloody. But when we look at this sacrifice through the lens of love, we see something different: We see power, self-control, ultimate victory, and salvation for all who believe.

Uncovering the lies you're told involves taking off the glasses of fear and putting on the glasses of love. These two kingdoms change how you see the circumstances around you. The kingdom perspective you are viewing your life through influences how you see yourself, but it also affects how you see God. The kingdom of darkness keeps us from seeing any hope in our lives. And often when we cry out for God in our very real pain, a lie may be keeping us from seeing just how close He really is.

TRACING GOD

Scripture

> From that time on Jesus began to explain to his disciples that he must go to Jerusalem and suffer many things at the hands of the elders, the chief priests and the teachers of the law, and that he must be killed and on the third day be raised to life.
>
> Peter took him aside and began to rebuke him. "Never, Lord!" he said. "This shall never happen to you!"
>
> Jesus turned and said to Peter, "Get behind me, Satan! You are a stumbling block to me; you do not

have in mind the concerns of God, but merely human concerns."

MATTHEW 16:21-23

Devotional

This Scripture used to be hard for me. I thought, *That seems a bit harsh, Jesus—Peter just wanted to protect you.* But Jesus saw that the kingdom of darkness was fueling Peter's words because they were spoken out of a lie fueled by fear masked as desire and concern. You see, many Hebrew people in that day had heard about a messiah who would bring salvation to the people of Israel. The Messiah was going to break them free from captivity. The people of Israel had been oppressed and abused for generations under Roman rule. And they were taught from a young age to hold on, be faithful, because the Messiah was coming.

And here Jesus was saying that He was going to be killed. The perspective that Peter was taught from childhood said nothing about the Messiah dying. I can only imagine the thoughts flying through Peter's mind . . . and even the fear of going back to life as usual, with no salvation, and no messiah. He was unable to accept the truth that Jesus was sharing because of what he'd been taught since childhood. Peter had not broken free from the false assumption that the Messiah he'd been told about was coming to rescue the Jews from Roman oppression. Instead, He was coming to rescue them from the far greater danger of sin and its eternal consequences. To help Peter fully embrace God's truth, Jesus wanted to separate him from a perspective that he had held for years. Jesus confronted that perspective with truth to break Peter (and any listeners) free from this doctrine.

Reflection Questions

1. What lies did you uncover from the activity in this chapter?
2. How often do you plan to do the activities in this chapter? Plan to revisit these exercises periodically to uncover any lies that have newly attempted to take root.
3. How do you think the lies accepted in our childhood affect our doctrine and belief about God?
4. Are there some areas of your life where you struggle to see hope because of a lie or a fear?

Prayer

Dear Lord, we thank You for the opportunity to continue this journey and uncover the lies that have affected our lives. We pray that as we begin the next section of this book You will help us see You at work in our lives. Help us come out of hiding, remove the masks and costumes, and throw out the lies, that we may hear and see You even in the unexpected places. In Jesus' name, amen!

Part 2

FINDING GOD

In part 1, we went on a journey of figuring out where we are in our emotional life, thought life, and relationship with God. You may have discovered that for years you have been hiding behind masks and costumes, afraid to show your brokenness. For us as Christians in this modern world, suffering may not seem synonymous with our walk with Christ. We might expect a big raise, a fancy car, and abundant health. Now that we have uncovered the reality of our broken hearts and shattered thoughts, the question *God, where are You?* may be even more pronounced. With a better sense of the extent of our suffering, the longing to know where God is in all this may have gotten even louder . . . and that's good. We will spend this section discovering where God is amid life's pain and unknowns.

CHAPTER BREAKDOWN

Let's look at an outline of what we'll cover in part 2.

Chapter 5 • Is That a Rhetorical Question?: Noticing God's Attributes and Kept Promises. We will explore the common tendency to wonder *God, where are You?* without truly expecting an answer. Often we pose this question out of frustration, grief, or confusion—more as a statement of despair than a genuine inquiry. But what if we shifted our posture and began to seek God's presence with intention and hope? This chapter challenges us to move from rhetorical lament to purposeful pursuit, encouraging us to believe that God can and does respond when we honestly and earnestly seek Him.

Chapter 6 ◆ The Darkness You Can Feel: God amid Abandonment, Rejection, and Hurt. We will consider how to find God when you have been rejected, abandoned, or abused by the very people you looked to for security and protection. "The darkness you can feel" refers to the loneliness that sets in deeply when you have suffered trauma from the hands of another human. Where is God when this happens? Is this just something that the devil makes happen to you while God sits at a distance?

Chapter 7 ◆ Drowning in Failure: God Is Near Even When We Fall Short. We will review how to find God when you feel like you have failed. Failure (or perceived failure) can cause its own turmoil in our lives. When we started a business and it failed, or got married and the relationship fell apart, or sinned after becoming a Christian . . . we can find ourselves wondering, *Where is God when we fail? Did He let us fail? Does He not want to be near us because we failed?* We will explore these questions and more.

Chapter 8 ◆ Finding God in the Storm: Seeing Clearly When Life Is Out of Control. We will learn how to find God when it feels like our lives are completely out of control. It's easy to question whether God is near when everything seems to be falling apart even when you are doing everything right: when you lose the job after getting a great review, or your home is washed away in a natural disaster, or your health is deteriorating, or your spouse passes away. In these raging storms it can feel difficult to find God.

GOALS OF THIS SECTION

In this section you will learn to

- understand the importance of actively looking for God;
- see God in places where you have experienced trauma at the hands of another person;
- see God in places where you feel like you have failed; and
- see God in places where your life feels like it's crumbling through no fault of your own.

After we opened up so many wounds in part 1, you may expect the next step would be to tend to the wounds and bandage them up. But when it comes to healing, step one is acknowledgment of the pain, and step two is identifying where the help is. God is our help, and before we attempt to bandage our wounds, we must locate where our help is, where God is amid our pain. Running from discomfort may have been your default setting for years, but it has also led you to years of hiding. Instead of running from discomfort, let us be okay with the discomfort while we seek God, our help and our hope.

5

IS THAT A RHETORICAL QUESTION?

Noticing God's Attributes and Kept Promises

I remember the first time I heard the word *rhetorical.* My mom was staring into my eyes, and she said, "Dominique, this is not a rhetorical question." Context clues helped me understand that my mom needed an answer. Sometimes parents ask a child questions when they're being disciplined, and the child knows they better not actually answer! But in that moment with my mother, the question she asked was one I knew I needed to find an answer to—and a good one at that.

I don't recall what I was in trouble for when she said that, but I remember quickly stammering out an answer . . . and learning the word *rhetorical.* In the human experience there are questions that we ask that we never intend to answer. Perhaps they are questions asked playfully and the answer is implied, or those really hard questions that no one knows the answer to, such as "What is the meaning of life?" We may ponder them, but we never expect to settle on an explicit answer.

God, where are You? is often treated like a rhetorical question. We ask it, oftentimes amid tears, but do we actively seek the answer? I remember asking the question expecting God to swoop in and show up like Batman does after seeing the Bat-Signal shining across the sky. But treating the question like a Bat-Signal implies that God was not already there. It's like a judgment statement: "God, You're not here when You should be."

For many years I didn't try to find God; I treated the question as rhetorical when it shouldn't have been. What would happen if we *actually* began to seek an answer to the question we are crying out?

In part 1 we spent time together uncovering where we are. Oftentimes we can't see God in our situation because we don't have a good perspective of where we are. Take the Pharisees and the Sadducees, for example. There they were, in the presence of Jesus—*God in the flesh*—and they didn't recognize Him! How is that even possible?

During that time Israel was under Roman rule. It was a tough situation to be in. The Pharisees and the Sadducees ran to their religious traditions to find God while they waited for the Messiah. The problem is that many took on religious traditions to wield power and therefore hide their vulnerability. Unlike the woman with the issue of blood, the woman at the well, or the father with the demon-possessed child, who weren't afraid to name their struggles and seek the help they needed, the Pharisees and Sadducees used religious traditions to cover their frailty in order to survive the harshness of Roman rule. And onto the scene steps Jesus, allowing people to come to Him with their brokenness.

In Mark 2:17 Jesus said, "It is not the healthy who need a doctor, but the sick. I have not come to call the righteous, but sinners." The tricky part of this is that before you recognize the doctor is in the room, you have to come to grips with the fact that you need a doctor. The Pharisees and Sadducees struggled to admit that they needed a doctor as much as the prostitutes and tax collectors they avoided in the streets. This is why part 1, "Finding Yourself," is so important. Much like the Pharisees, we can't see Jesus when we don't even see where we are.

Once you realize that you need a doctor, the next step is to look for one. The woman with the issue of blood went out and looked for Jesus amid her brokenness. The man with the demon-possessed son went out and looked for Jesus while his life was falling apart. The Roman official with the dying daughter went out and looked for Jesus in his despair. When we ask the question *God, where are You?* we have two options: (1) we can conclude that God is not here, or (2) we can look for Him. This chapter is calling us to choose the latter option. Look for God in your past and current brokenness, in your frailty and vulnerability.

This section is about learning how to look for God, learning how to see Him in places we may have never thought He was. When we call out, "God, where are You?" and don't expect an answer, it's because we secretly think, *He's not here.* But intentionally looking for God causes us to suspend that judgment and consider for a moment, *Maybe, just maybe, He's closer than I think.*

HOW DO I FIND HIM?

A lot of people struggle to find God because they cannot physically see Him. They think, *How can I have a relationship with someone I cannot see?* I often think of a person who is blind. Those who cannot see with their eyes use their other senses to experience their environment. Just because they can't physically see the world doesn't mean that it isn't present. When one of our senses is impaired, we use our other senses to "see" the person who was there all along.

That is exactly what I began to learn during some of my darkest moments; how to "see" God even when the circumstances made the feat seem impossible. I had to accept that I was not seeing the full picture before I could learn other methods to "see" and experience God's attributes.

When we are not looking for God, we often miss parts of His character. I will share the five attributes of God's character that I found myself constantly looking for to identify Him in my circumstances. A child who is blind knows his own mother from any other woman. How is that possible when he can't physically see her? He uses other attributes to identify her. He knows the sound of her voice, the length of her fingers, and the width of her waist. The types of intimate attributes that are more apparent when we are in a consistent relationship with someone are what I began to look for even when I found it challenging to "see" God.

GOD'S ATTRIBUTES

When life feels uncertain, one of the most grounding truths we can hold on to is the unchanging character of God. His attributes aren't just theological concepts—they are steady and faithful, and they shape how He interacts with us and how we experience His presence. In this section, we'll explore key attributes of God that reveal His heart and His character.

Attribute 1: Love

The love of God has become a relatively taboo topic. People talk about God's love as if it is some type of passive feeling of pleasantness; perhaps that's why we miss this attribute in our lives. God's love is His state of being and can also be understood as a collection of decisions listed in 1 Corinthians 13. This Scripture states:

> Love is patient, love is kind. It does not envy, it does not boast, it is not proud. It does not dishonor others, it is not self-seeking, it is not easily angered, it keeps no record of wrongs. Love does not delight in evil but rejoices with the truth. It always protects, always trusts, always hopes, always perseveres.
>
> Love never fails.
>
> 1 CORINTHIANS 13:4-8

Paying attention to where God's love—the kind described in 1 Corinthians 13—shows up in my life has helped me recognize His presence, even in seasons that feel dark and uncertain. I see His love when a friend checks in when I feel alone, offering patience and understanding without judgment. I feel it when my spouse offers grace instead of criticism after I fall short, or when someone believes in me even when I'm doubting myself. Sometimes it's in a quiet text that reminds me I'm not forgotten, or a kind word that lifts a weight I didn't realize I was carrying. These moments reflect the kind of love that is patient, kind, not self-seeking—love that protects, trusts, hopes, and perseveres. When I feel that kind of love directed toward me, I know it's more than coincidence—it's God, reaching into my life through others, reminding me that even here, even now, I am seen and loved.

Attribute 2: Instruction

In times of struggle I tend to search for God's strength. I want Him to fix the situation. If someone is being mean to me, I want the lion in God to be released and scare them away. If my life is falling apart, I want God's strength to hold all the bricks together. But in my constant seeking for His power, I miss God's instruction. Throughout the Scriptures we see God instructing His people, teaching them how to live holy and set apart. God was constantly showing His people what it looked like to follow Him. Let us not neglect looking for God's instruction even in circumstances that we want Him to take away. God's instruction can be found through studying the Bible, in quiet moments of prayer, and in spiritual disciplines that draw us nearer to Him.

Attribute 3: Faithfulness

I'll be honest, this attribute was one of the hardest for me to understand. For a long time, I believed that God's faithfulness meant He would respond to my every desire, especially the things I wanted day to day. But as I studied the Scriptures more deeply, I came to realize that God isn't faithful to our fleeting wants, emotions, or cravings. He is faithful to *Himself*—to His Word, His promises, and His purposes for our lives. This is a good thing because God's mission and promises are for the good of those who love Him; they don't change with the wind like human lusts and desires. God's faithfulness is also what makes Him so trustworthy. He is faithful to His promises and to His mission. Understanding what those things are helps us find God amid life's circumstances. Keep reading, as I will unpack some of His promises and mission later in this chapter.

Attribute 4: Foresight

God sees more than we could ever imagine. He sees our heart. He sees the future. He properly sees the past and the present. Because of His foresight, God is constantly preparing us for where He is guiding us. I think of Joseph's story often. So many of his circumstances seemed so cruel and at the hands of his own brothers, but those circumstances, although difficult, were opportunities to prepare Joseph for what God knew the world would need: provision during famine.

Attribute 5: Power

We can't leave out God's power—it's one of the attributes we look for most often. In times of crisis, uncertainty, or need, we long to see God move in visible, undeniable ways. We look for His power to heal, to protect, to save. And yes, these are beautiful and powerful proofs of His presence.

But if we don't see these outward signs, we can easily miss the many other ways God's power is at work. He also sustains us, strengthens us right where we are, and holds us together when everything feels like it's falling apart. God's power isn't always revealed through a changed circumstance—sometimes, it shows up most profoundly through a changed *you.*

Think about it. Maybe you've witnessed a family member recover from an illness that doctors said was impossible to cure. Or you've seen a friend's life radically transformed after they came to faith. Maybe you've experienced unexplainable peace in the middle of a storm or found strength to keep going when you had nothing left. These, too, are signs of God's power at work.

• • •

In the next few chapters we are going to look for where God was in some of the most challenging circumstances in our lives. Easier said than done. We will find that God was there in our darkest times, which sounds awesome, but this was one of the most painful points of my faith journey. Recognizing God's presence was reassuring, but realizing He could have changed the situation but didn't was crushing.

As you navigate these next few chapters, you may feel that tension: gratitude that God has always been there and grief that He didn't rescue you from the hardest parts of your story.

You could put this book down right now and continue to ask a rhetorical *God, where are You?* . . . hoping that doing so will encourage God to sweep in and fix your circumstance. Or you can take my hand and together we can look for God in the hardest moments of life. It's up to you, but I encourage you to continue exploring the bigger picture. Finding God in the crevices of your story where you felt most alone is a journey worth taking.

So what do you say?

Since you have continued reading, I'll assume that you want to keep going. Let's do this. Remember, tears are okay. If ever you need to take a break from this book, you can. I will never tell you that this journey is easy, but I will continue to remind you that it's worth it!

GOD'S MISSION AND PROMISES

If you could not find a loved one, you would likely begin looking for them based on what they like, places they frequent, and the type of person they are. If it was a child, you may search where their favorite toys are or run to the playground down the street. If it was your spouse, you would call their best friend or drive by their favorite restaurant. The best map for finding a missing loved one is created by recalling who they are. The same is true for God. What we know to be true about God is the best map for finding Him when it seems too dark and challenging to see Him or feel His presence.

Knowing God's mission and promises can help us find God in our past and present circumstances. God never strays away from either. He is faithful to what He says; therefore what He's said is the best way to understand where He is. Let's uncover the mission of God a bit by diving into His Word.

In Revelation 5 we get a glimpse into why God sacrificed His Son, Jesus, which is deeply tied to God's overall mission. John has just seen the Lamb who was slain appear in the throne room of God. We understand that this slain Lamb represents Jesus, and what happens in verses 8-10 reveals God's mission. It says:

> When [the Lamb] had taken [the scroll], the four living creatures and the twenty-four elders fell down before the Lamb. Each one had a harp and they were holding golden bowls full of incense, which are the prayers of God's people. And they sang a new song, saying:
>
> "You are worthy to take the scroll
> and to open its seals,
> because you were slain,
> and with your blood you purchased for God
> persons from every tribe and language and
> people and nation.
> You have made them to be a kingdom and priests to
> serve our God,
> and they will reign on the earth."
>
> **REVELATION 5:8-10**

The sacrifice of Jesus was about more than just saving us from our sins (although that's important!). It was about more than eternal life for humanity. It was also about God's mission to establish a diverse Kingdom of many languages, people, and nations who would gather to serve God for the good of all on earth.

Revelation 21 shows us what it is like to live in that Kingdom. John shares the prophecy given to him:

> I heard a loud voice from the throne saying, "Look! God's dwelling place is now among the people, and he will dwell with them. They will be his people, and God himself will be with them and be their God. 'He will wipe every tear from their eyes. There will be no more death' or mourning or crying or pain, for the old order of things has passed away."
>
> He who was seated on the throne said, "I am making everything new!" Then he said, "Write this down, for these words are trustworthy and true."
>
> **REVELATION 21:3-5**

In both passages from Revelation we learn God's mission is to bring humanity to Himself as citizens of His diverse Kingdom. As King, He will give His people peace and joy, wipe away every tear, and protect them from all harm. We know God's wonderful plan for us as His Kingdom people, yet we also know this place without crying or pain is not our current reality. In the midst of life's ups and downs, we can rest assured that God has not abandoned His good plan. When we look, we can see evidence of God drawing us to Himself even as we cry out for Him.

Have you ever been in a hard situation that led you closer to God? Remember, God's mission is to draw humans to Himself. So when we draw near to God even amid life's tragedies, we find evidence of His presence. Because where His mission is present, God is also present. We also see that His promise across generations is based on the truth that we will find everything we need in God (2 Corinthians 9:8; Philippians 4:19). The truest thing about us is that we are beloved children of God, His Kingdom people. So when we find ourselves pressing into God in difficult situations, we can rest assured that God is in our midst.

Why are we talking about God's attributes, mission, and promises? Because as we explore our tragedies and traumas, we will use what we know about who God is to find Him in moments where we didn't know He was there.

In the next few chapters we will explore three types of circumstances that we may find difficult to find God in: when we feel abandoned, when we fall short, and when life seems out of control. We will use what we know about God to learn how to find Him in life's sufferings and challenges.

TRACING GOD

Scripture

> We walk by faith, not by sight.
>
> 2 CORINTHIANS 5:7, ESV

Devotional

In his second letter to the believers at Corinth, Paul shares that life involves suffering but that believers can find comfort and hope in faith. Challenges will come during our time on earth, but even so we can continue to live for God.

Walking by faith is not about figuring out the right prayer to get God to do whatever you want Him to do. Walking by faith does not involve a ten-step process to health and wealth. Walking by faith is about knowing how to find God even when life is so hard that you can't see or feel Him. Walking by faith is about holding on to what you know and not giving it up for what you don't know. For example, I may not know when a particular personal storm will end, but I do know that God is trustworthy and that He has a plan. I may not know how this situation will work out, but I do know that God causes all things to work together for the good of those who love Him (Romans 8:28).

Walking by faith is not about making everything work out the way I want. Rather, it is about learning to find God amid suffering and cling to Him even in my darkest experiences.

Reflection Questions

1. Why do you think it's important to find God in the pain of your past?
2. Which of God's attributes resonates with you the most right now, and why?
3. How do you sense God inviting you to participate in His mission and purpose for your life in this season?

4. When do you find it is most difficult to find God, and what do you think contributes to that feeling?

Prayer

Dear Lord, help us find You even when we can't see You. Help us identify Your presence even if we can't feel it. Call to our remembrance what we know about You, God, even as we revisit experiences where we felt like You were not with us. Teach us how to find You in the pain of the past so that we can find You in the challenges of today and the trials of tomorrow. In Jesus' name, amen!

6

THE DARKNESS YOU CAN FEEL

God amid Abandonment, Rejection, and Hurt

I used to hate sleeping in the dark. Even as a college student, when my roommate wasn't there I would turn the lights on when I went to bed. I could feel the darkness, and it didn't feel good. It felt suffocating and isolating and sometimes like it was hiding something or someone I could not see.

One time in college I walked a few blocks to my dorm in the dark. I felt unprepared for a nighttime stroll. I had no reflective clothing on, the area I had to walk through was not well lit, and I could see no one—and I mean no one—anywhere around. I started off at a leisurely pace but soon enough found myself sprinting across the campus.

I felt vulnerable and alone in the dark. It was my top priority to find a better-lit, more populated place where I could feel safe. The same thing can happen in our lives, and it often happens with other people. The presence of loved ones can light up your life. Hanging out with my husband or chatting on the phone with my best friend brings light and a feeling of safety. But people can also bring a feeling of darkness when they abandon, reject, or otherwise hurt you.

The feelings you experienced as a little girl trying to go to sleep in a dark room can rush in when someone rejects, abandons, or otherwise hurts your adult self. The dark room where you felt isolated and vulnerable then is similar to the areas of your life where you feel rejected, abandoned, and hurt now. These moments can be extremely traumatic and affect the way that we show up in our own life, trying to navigate around the places where people have chosen to bring darkness instead of light to a situation or relationship.

The loneliness and vulnerability I felt while sprinting across my college campus and as a little girl lying in my dark room crying out to my parents is similar to what our grown-up self feels when we're rejected, abandoned, and betrayed at the hands of another. Whether it is someone you know deeply or someone you have no relationship with, people can often cause great pain in others' lives. And that pain can feel isolating as we attempt to navigate it.

Before I started actively looking for God in my pain, I noticed at church I would never hear people talk about the tragedy, trials, and trauma that they had experienced. And if I did hear them briefly mention those painful experiences, it was only to then describe how God miraculously came through and turned the circumstance around. Very rarely did I hear about the messy middle, the season where things weren't working out and God hadn't miraculously turned things around. Very rarely did I hear anyone talk about how to find God when you couldn't seem to find your way out of darkness.

I wondered whether God was with me in the dark moments or whether He only showed up to clean up the mess that trauma left behind. I struggled to connect with God in hardship because I didn't know if He wanted to be there with me amid the mess. It wasn't until later that I understood that God was with me the whole time. And the same is true for you in your pain. I want you to know you are not alone. We are navigating this together. Our dark moments may look different, but we need to process and find God within them. So in the next few chapters I am going to vulnerably open up the pages of my life as you look for God in your own heart-wrenching moments.

Let's start. I have tissues next to me. I hope you have some, too, because I have a feeling we're going to need them.

YOUR DARKEST MOMENTS

Think about a moment in your life that felt dark and lonely. A time you felt rejected, abandoned, or deeply hurt by another. As beings made in the image of the Light of the World, we can carry light into other people's lives. But when we let our sinful nature win, we can take away the light in other people's lives. Pain felt at the hands of another is one of the greatest we can know.

I want you to revisit one of your darkest moments. If it

feels like too much, pause, breathe, and consider going for a walk, calling a friend, and possibly scheduling a session with a therapist for help navigating the memory. If more than one moment is coming to mind, do not overwhelm your system by attempting to deal with them all in one day. Choose one per day to process thoroughly. Use the same moment as you journey through this chapter. Then revisit this chapter when you are ready to uncover another issue.

When you are ready to dive in, let's navigate these steps:

1. What is one moment where you felt alone, abandoned, rejected, or otherwise deeply hurt by another person?
2. Describe this moment in detail.
3. Evaluate how it made you feel.
4. Identify an area where you notice it affecting your life.

I'll start.

My parents were married for nearly twenty-five years before getting divorced. I never remember them having a great relationship; they argued a lot. On the surface, their divorce came as a bit of a relief. It wasn't until a recent therapy session that I realized how difficult that time was for me. I had attempted to move on with my life without processing the events that took place. Little did I know that I experienced my parents' divorce as abandonment.

While their divorce came as no surprise, I was significantly affected by what happened toward the end of their marriage. My father was my hero. Many people I knew did not have a father who was active in their lives; some didn't even know who their father was. So I was among the privileged few who not only had a father in the home but also one who was involved in his child's life. He was my math tutor, the one who taught me to drive. I wanted to marry a man just like my dad. I never could imagine that my dad would do anything to hurt anyone. My mom would often claim that my dad was cheating on her. I was so upset with my mom for talking about *my hero* this way. One day I asked him, "Have you ever cheated on Mom?" He looked me in the eye and said no. I knew it!

Imagine my surprise to learn that my dad had actually had an affair. *WAIT, WHAT? No way! He told me that he had never done this. He looked me in the eye. He lied?* I attempted to move on from this information as if nothing had happened, but I was crumbling inside. It affected my ability to focus in school and my relationships, and it drew a wedge between my father and me for ten years. I stopped talking to him about my life. I stopped asking him for advice. If my hero had lied to me about this, I wondered what else he lied about. This darkness produced a shadow over even the beautiful moments of my life. During this time I graduated from college, got married, and moved to a new state, but it felt like I was walking through all these experiences in quicksand, sinking at every step.

Now that you've seen an example, it's your turn. What is one dark moment in your life where you felt alone, abandoned, rejected, or otherwise deeply hurt by another person?

Grab your journal and write about the moment in detail. You don't have to hold back. (Chances are, you have been holding back for a while.) Now is the time to share—in detail—about your experience. Don't feel the need to rush to the next section of this chapter until you are ready. Finding God in the dark places of your life can be quite a painful process, but it is also beautiful: Some of the things that have been trapped in your heart and mind for a long time are finally able to come out.

We spent time describing what happened; now let's dive into how this event made you feel. You may find it more difficult to express what you're feeling than to describe the dark moment. I often find myself expressing my opinions as feelings because I struggle to identify my feelings. My therapist and my husband both often say, "Dominique, that is not a feeling. Let's walk together to find the feeling." I spent years shoving down painful moments and the feelings that were attached to them. Because of that, when I started searching for God in my darkest moments, I was very detached from my feelings. I began to reference feelings wheels and charts to help me to uncover my feelings.

I encourage you to use the Feelings Wheel that follows to identify the specific feelings you are experiencing.[4]

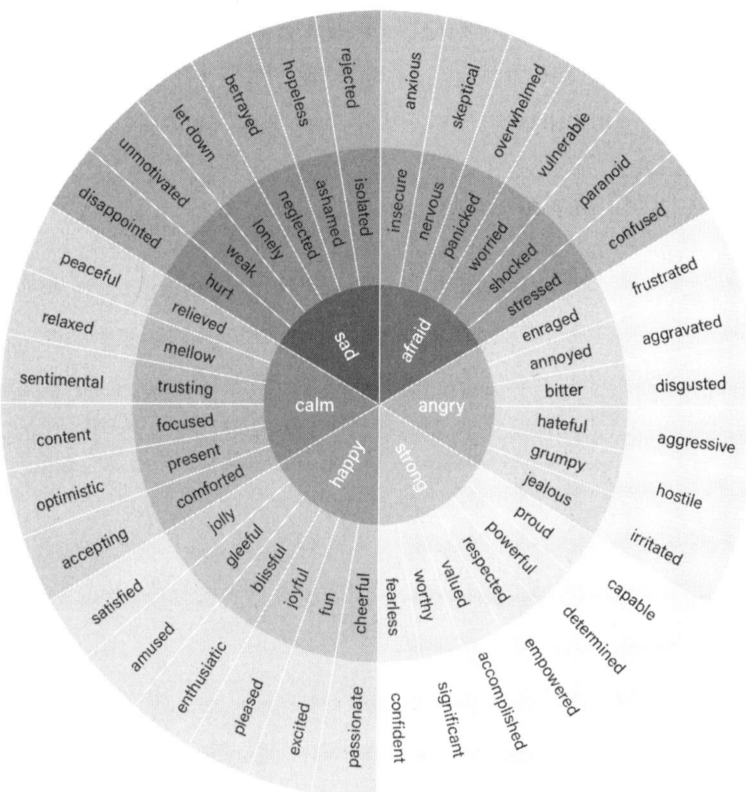

The way the wheel works is that the closer you are to the center, the more basic the feeling is. (This center section is a great place to start when you're untangling complex emotions.) As you head to the middle section you become a bit more specific, and then the outer circle is the most specific. The more specific you can get, the better. And it is okay to identify multiple feelings, because multiple feelings tend to be attached to the difficult moments in our lives.

I'll start.

After the situation with my dad, the first feelings I identified were sadness and anger. But as I used the Feelings Wheel, I realized that beneath the anger, I actually felt let down and betrayed. And beneath the sadness, I was really feeling hurt and disappointed.

This might surprise you—some of the feelings I ended up naming came from different areas of the wheel than where I started. That's a helpful reminder: As you reflect more deeply, your emotions may shift or become clearer, and you might discover that what you're really feeling lives in a completely different emotional category than you first thought. That's okay—and it's part of the process.

In fact, emotions like anger can sometimes act as a mask, covering up more vulnerable feelings like fear, sadness, or shame.[5] So if your emotional journey takes a few turns as you go deeper, let it. That's how you get closer to what's really going on inside.

Now it's your turn: What feelings did you experience during and after this situation? I have found that many people do not express their feelings. We may shove the feelings down, or we may act on the feelings (by lashing out, screaming, or cursing, for example). But how often do we share what we are feeling by saying, "I feel sad," and then examine this sadness and realize it is actually a deep hurt and disappointment? Or saying, "I feel angry," and then explore that feeling and discover it's actually betrayal?

I encourage you to put words to your feelings. Even if you don't feel that way now, let's explore what you felt in the dark moment you're processing. Take your time. Use the Feelings Wheel if you need to, and put words to your feelings.

THE IMPACT ON YOUR LIFE

Lastly, we are going to identify the areas of our lives this situation has affected.

I'll start.

The painful situation with my father affected my life in a variety of ways. I will share the five I have identified. It took me quite some time to recognize these far-reaching effects.

1. *This situation affected the way I show up in my relationship with my husband.* For a long time I found myself paying attention to what he was watching on social media and who he was calling on his phone. I felt extremely insecure.
2. *The situation affected my relationship with my father.* He was no longer my hero, and I found it extremely difficult to determine who he is in my life if he no longer fit in that role.
3. *The situation affected the way I sought sound counsel.* I was much slower to seek advice after learning my dad had lied to me. When I did receive advice, I was extremely critical of the person offering it. It was hard to trust that others' advice was reliable because my dad, whom I had trusted, had given me advice that I later found out did not align with his actions.

4. *The situation affected the way I saw people.* I began to feel extremely vulnerable around people I was close to. My experience with my dad seemed to indicate that it was easier for people you love to deceive you than people you aren't in close relationship with, so I put distance between me and my closest relationships to better see my loved ones' intentions toward me.

5. *The situation affected the way I interacted with God.* This area was the hardest one for me to admit. My earthly father had betrayed my trust, and I felt that my heavenly Father had done the same. God didn't protect me from the pain, and He didn't shield my father from his own actions. So I began to go to God only for tasks He wanted me to complete. Our relationship became transactional—I placed the relational part on the shelf.

Whew! Those were tough things to admit; however, this is a necessary step in the journey to find God in our darkest moments.

So now it is your turn. What other areas of your life has this situation influenced? I found it difficult to uncover these things, so I asked these questions:

- *In what areas have I felt similar feelings* before *the situation I'm examining happened?* For example, there have been times when I've felt betrayed and disappointed seemingly without any cause for this response. In what areas have you felt those same feelings strongly *before* there was an action to trigger these responses?

- *When have my responses felt bigger than the situation called for?* What might those moments reveal about deep wounds or unresolved pain? In what ways did you promise to protect yourself after the situation? (Often when we are hurt, we make secret promises to ourselves, such as *I will never let another man hurt me like this one did.*) And then begin to uncover how you have been keeping this secret promise.

Take your time to uncover your pain from this situation. Please know that you can move as slowly as you need to through these questions. Don't feel like you need to rush; you don't. Take your time.

GOD, WHERE ARE YOU?

Now let's dig into the questions we have been waiting for. *God, where were You in this dark situation where I felt abandoned and rejected by this person? God, where were You when I experienced this pain?* Understanding where God was in past pain will help us understand where He may be in our present pain. Is He aloof and disconnected? Is He far off, waiting for us to catch up? Is He in heaven working on a counterattack to the devil? Or is He close?

We will use what we know about God's attributes, mission, and promises to identify Him in the dark circumstance we're examining. We're going to look for God in the situation itself, in the events surrounding the situation, in the people connected to you during the situation, and in your life after the situation. You may not be able to find Him immediately, and that's okay. It takes some searching. There may be places where you cry out, "God, I can't find You; help me."

For this next step in the process, ask yourself the following questions:

1. Where can I find the attributes of God (love, patience, faithfulness, foresight, power, etc.) at work in this situation, in the events surrounding it, in the people connected to me during this time, and in the path of my life afterward?
2. Where can I find the promises of God at work in this situation, in the events surrounding it, in the people connected to me during this time, and in the path of my life afterward? (Consider promises God has made, whether they've been fulfilled yet or not.)
3. Where can I find the mission of God at work in this situation, in the events surrounding it, in the people connected to me during this time, and in the path of my life afterward? (Remember, God's mission is to draw us close to Him, to get rid of any lies or anything else that keeps us distant from Him.)

You may find God's attributes in a person who was there as you were navigating the situation. You may find His promises flooding your mind as you sit in your room crying. You may find His mission of drawing you close happens as you pray more than before.

Can you identify God's attributes on display even in your darkest moment or its aftermath? Can you find His promises on display or a promise spoken at that moment? Can you see Him drawing you close during the situation or in subsequent events?

You can answer "I don't know" to some of the questions, but I encourage you to look for God as much as you can in the dark moment we're revisiting together. Don't continue reading until you have attempted to answer these questions.

Where did you find God? Did He show up only when everything worked out? Was there evidence of His presence even when it was hard? Was there evidence that He was with you in the struggle?

One of the places I was shocked to see God in my challenging situation was in the destruction of an idol. I didn't realize that I had held my dad up as an idol in my life and that this was deeply affecting my relationship with God. As I dug deeper, I discovered that I didn't truly have a relationship with God during my time elevating my dad as a hero. I didn't have space for two heroes in my life. One of God's attributes is truth (John 14:6). He allows truth to be revealed and shared. God allowed the truth to be revealed about my dad's actions. The truth revealed was painful, but it was also evidence of God's hand. The shattering of my idol-like relationship with my father was deeply painful, but it also aligned with God's mission to draw me close to Him. I would never have been able to get there relationally if my earthly father was in that space. I also realized that God set my father free from my expectations and perspective so that he could get free himself. As long as he lived in a lie to preserve my view of him, my earthly father was unable to heal. And in God's grace and mercy, he restored my relationship with my father to be more beautiful, honest, and healthy than before.

As we begin to see God's attributes, promises, and mission, we can be assured that He is with us amid rejection, abandonment, and loneliness. God is with us in the darkness. Now that we understand that God is with us in our darkest moments, we may be wondering: *Is He with me while I am drowning?* (We'll cover that in chapter 7.) *Is He with me amid the storms of life?* (We'll cover that in chapter 8.) And *If He is with me in my hardest moments, why doesn't He stop them from happening?* (We'll cover that in part 3.)

As we navigate the difficult terrain of the hardships in our lives, we may be surprised where we find God's attributes, promises, and mission revealed. This is further proof that when we cannot see Him or feel His power, we must intentionally seek God. As we do, we'll discover God demonstrating His loving presence with His people, time and time again.

TRACING GOD

Scripture

> [Joseph said,] "As for you, you meant evil against me; but God meant it for good, in order to bring it about as it is this day, to save many people alive."
>
> **GENESIS 50:20,** NKJV

Devotional

Genesis 50:20 recounts what Joseph told his brothers about their mistreatment of him. (They had thrown him into a pit and then sold him into slavery.) He initially found favor in slavery, but when his master's wife lied, he was wrongfully thrown into prison. Joseph then found himself experiencing favor in prison, and he accurately interpreted dreams for two important members of the pharaoh's staff. Joseph had asked one of them to remember him when he was restored to his position as cupbearer, but that person promptly forgot Joseph when his circumstances improved.

Joseph knew a thing or two about being abandoned, rejected, and hurt by others. He knew what it was like to feel alone. But Joseph also learned to seek God in dark circumstances. He spoke the message found in Genesis 50:20 after he had been elevated to second-in-command in Egypt to save the Egyptians and their neighbors (including Joseph's family) from a famine.

Joseph recognized that although what he was going through was hard, God was right there with him every step of the way. Although others' intentions toward him were bad, God was there for Joseph. God didn't come at the end of the issue and say, "Oh, I better clean this up." God was there each step, allowing events to unfold for the good and protecting him in the most challenging of times.

Even in our darkest moments, God is there. We must intentionally seek Him in order to calm our minds enough to realize He is not far off. And if God is right there with us in our pain, then we can rest assured that He has a plan, He has a purpose, and our struggles won't be in vain. They will be for the good and for His glory. Joseph went through years of trials, but God's hand was with him. No matter how scary the dark places feel, God is not afraid of the dark.

Reflection Questions

1. What are some other Bible stories where you see God with someone in situations of betrayal, abandonment, and/or rejection?
2. What do those stories teach you about God amid dark places?
3. What are some limitations in yourself or your knowledge when it comes to finding God in dark places or identifying His character, promises, or mission?
4. How will you address limitations in your knowledge of who God is and who He has been throughout history?

Prayer

Dear Lord, help us continue to see You in dark places. I pray that You help us learn how to seek You using past events so that when new rejection, abandonment, or betrayal comes, we can find Your presence in the midst of it and know we are safe. In Jesus' name, amen!

7

DROWNING IN FAILURE

God Is Near Even When We Fall Short

I remember one time I went to the pool with my friends. All my friends were like fish in the water. They knew how to swim in shallow and deep water, and they jumped into the pool without hesitation. I, on the other hand, don't know how to swim. So I gradually made my way into the shallow end of the pool. I chose a space that I knew I could be successful in since swimming was not really my thing, but I loved being in water. At five feet four inches tall, I felt quite confident and comfortable about my skills in the shallow end.

I splashed around and had fun as I watched my friends racing back and forth from the shallow end of the pool to the deep end. I had decided that today I would become comfortable putting my head under water because I figured that was the first step to learning how to swim. I was quite confident that in three feet of water, I was safe and had the skills needed to navigate these waters. So I began to jump up and down. Every time I went down I put my head under water, and every time I jumped up I breathed in fresh air. I did this about five times, but on the sixth time I couldn't find my way up. My skills didn't seem to be working, and I was afraid to open my eyes, so I began flailing my arms in hopes I would flail my way back to oxygen.

The lifeguard probably thought I was joking because he saw how tall I was and how confidently I had bobbed in and out of the water five times before. It was one of my friends who pulled me out of the water. I quickly got out of the pool and walked to one of the chairs, terrified that I had almost drowned, grateful for my friend's help, and embarrassed because it was only three feet of water. I was shaken up and felt like a failure. I had mapped out the circumstances just right. I attempted submersing my head in water five times before. Why did I fail the sixth time? Why weren't my skills and the circumstances I so carefully curated enough to keep me from almost drowning? Why did I need someone else to rescue me? Why did I fail? I had no answers. Fear set in, and I did not go back into the water that day.

Drowning can happen in other areas of our lives. We have curated an environment for success. We are ready and able . . . and the next thing we know, we are drowning. It can feel like failure when our skills aren't enough and we can't seem to reach the expectations and goals we set for ourselves. And we may be so overcome by fear that we refuse to try again and instead go sit in a more comfortable area and watch others enjoy their lives. The way we process—or don't process—failure in our lives has a very deep impact.

LEARNING FROM FAILURE

How do you process failure? Do you ignore it as if nothing happened and press on to the next task? Do you crumble at the first sign of failure? Does it change how you make decisions and interact with others? Often we talk about seeing God in the obvious blessings and successful moments in our lives but don't talk about the times when we feel like we failed. Now it's time to talk about failure. When we discuss difficult or traumatic moments, we tend to share about when people betrayed or otherwise hurt us. We talk about when people turned their back on us and rejected us or about situations that were out of our control. But we rarely talk about the moments of failure. The moments when we felt like we let ourselves, God, and everyone around us down. We don't often share about those moments being painful and traumatic, but they are.

After a failure, we typically do one of two things: (1) We beat ourselves up, or (2) we shove every emotion down, dust ourselves off, and keep going. (I've done both at various times.) Today we are going to intentionally return to moments where we felt like we failed and look for God. Although we are doing this one situation at a time, you can come back to these chapters over and over to identify in past or present situations where God is amid life's hardest moments and to process your repressed emotions, thoughts, and feelings. These reflective activities help you identify where you are and then locate

God in your midst. Both are necessary as you process life's circumstances.

We will use a process similar to the one we employed in chapter 6 because that is what helped me walk through the pain and emotions of my most difficult moments. I am not an expert on navigating traumatic experiences. I am writing this book because I am on this journey myself and I am learning so much that I pray will be helpful to you along the way.

Strategic reflection is not meant to be the be-all and end-all to your journey, but it will encourage you to acknowledge and identify your feelings instead of shoving them down. As you learn to process your feelings in healthy ways, you will find that God is not far off even when you feel like you failed.

This book is not a magic wand to summon God's power and get your hard circumstances to cease and comfort to come. Seeking God does not stop the hard, contrary to popular modern doctrine. Finding God where you least expected Him to be calms your heart and mind, and helps you stand a bit steadier in your faith when hardship comes. Notice I said *when*, not *if.* The practices you learn here can be used throughout your life. Future challenges will emerge, and when they do, I pray that these reflection activities will help you process and provide perspective.

In chapter 6 we journeyed through four key steps to evaluating a moment where we felt abandoned, rejected, or otherwise hurt by others.

In this chapter, we'll use similar steps to focus on a time we felt like we failed. I know that often we do not want to revisit these memories because they can be painful. However, if we do not process the failure and find God in it, the experience will sit in our hearts, dictating the decisions we make and the risks we take. Unprocessed failure can morph into fear, a fear that grips you anytime you attempt something new.

We will look at one failure in your life and follow four steps. Take this at your own pace and make room to truly, deeply reflect. (Remember, you can return to this chapter as needed to process other failures.)

Since we have been in this process of vulnerable sharing, I will start. I'll share a time in my life that I failed and walk you through my process of reflection and the journey of finding God in my failure.

The four steps have changed a bit, but not much. When you are ready, let's dive in:

1. *What is one moment where you felt like you failed?* The *Merriam-Webster Dictionary* defines *failure* as "a failing to perform a duty or expected action," "a state of inability to perform a normal function," and "a fracture or giving way under stress."[6] We have all failed at some point in our lives. We may have called failure by another name to lessen the blow (*I didn't fail; I just learned*). And while much of what we say to ourselves to move forward from failure is encouraging, the truth is that we failed, and failure can hurt. We may not have processed the pain or disappointment of past failures yet, which can keep us from moving forward in faith, taking healthy risks that help us grow. To start, identify a failure that comes to mind.

2. *Describe this moment in detail.* Who wants to describe failure in detail? I know I don't. But taking time to give words to the experience is a powerful point of the process. Don't back down from it.

3. *Evaluate how it made you feel.* Have you ever thought about how this failure made you feel initially, or did you just jump straight to the next thought? Taking the time to identify how you felt helps you understand yourself and gives you a truer picture for finding God's hand within your situation.

4. *Identify an area where you notice it affecting your life.* How has this moment of failure or a resulting fear of future failure affected your life? Your decisions? Your relationships?

I will start. May my sharing encourage you in yours. Feel free to go into even more detail than I do. I have a word count that I cannot go over in this book, but you don't. So reflect with as many words, illustrations, or tears as you need.

When I was a sophomore in college, I started a nonprofit organization called Project Dream BIG. I had high hopes for this organization, and I was convinced that when I graduated from college it would be my career. But we did not have funding for the organization to hire me so I began teaching. I shifted my dream a bit and figured I would teach for a little while and then eventually begin to work in the organization that I founded. Instead of that happening, I ended up discontinuing Project Dream BIG after the birth of my first child. I smiled and said that this was the best decision, but inside I felt like a quitter. I felt Project Dream BIG's closure was my fault.

You may need to revisit the Feelings Wheel, and that is okay. Sometimes it can be difficult to identify feelings when you are used to shoving them down. The Feelings Wheel can be found on page 87.

When Project Dream BIG ended, I felt sad, fearful, and angry. As I used the Feelings Wheel to really dig into these emotions, I realized that I felt guilty and ashamed, insecure and inadequate, and let down and resentful.

In what areas do I see this instance of fear affecting my life? The answer is everywhere! I don't like to experience the strong feelings of inadequacy and guilt that arose from what I perceived as my failure with Project Dream BIG, and I notice that in many different areas of my life.

As an adult I have avoided trying various activities, making new friends, and attempting new businesses or hobbies not because I was afraid of failure but because the post-failure feelings that I've experienced were so unpleasant. I began to believe I would prefer not doing anything so I didn't run the risk of feeling them.

In many instances the experience of failing is so traumatic that it etches itself into our heart and mind. And with every painful moment that embeds itself in our way of being, a familiar question bubbles up. *God, where are You when I fail? God, where are You when I am navigating disappointment? God, where are You when I am navigating resentment?*

It can be easy to believe that God is not near us when we fall short. Why would God want to be with us in our failures?

Questions like this will cause us to pull away from the idea that God could be anywhere close. And when we believe that our circumstance is one God cannot be near, we strive to make it appear like we haven't missed the mark. Cognitive dissonance will remind us of the truth, and we will attempt to push it down to live in a more comfortable version of reality. But what if we find God not by running from our failure but rather processing it, and looking for Him within and around it?

That may sound crazy, but let's give it a try. It's your turn to consider a time you failed. Pay attention to the first experience of failure that comes to your mind. I encourage you to spend time reflecting on these steps. Go as deep in your reflection as you are willing to.

Here are the steps:

1. What is one moment where you felt like you failed?
2. Describe this moment in detail.
3. Evaluate how it made you feel.
4. Identify an area where you notice it affecting your life.

Take out your journal and respond to each prompt. I know I have said it multiple times, but don't rush. There is no award for the fastest person to finish this book. (And even if there were, would you want it if it came at the cost of clarity, peace, and evidence of God's presence in the hardest moments of your life?)

GOD, WHERE ARE YOU?

The title of this book is the question that we are boldly asking as we uncover some of the most difficult moments of our lives. Instead of asking this question in passing, let's lean into it and find God in the most unexpected places.

In chapter 6 we looked for God's attributes, promises, and mission—and we saw God working in the hardest seasons of our lives. But could the same be true for the seasons and circumstances when the difficulties are our fault? Could God truly be in circumstances that we caused? Could His presence be seen in the failures that plague our hearts and minds? The only way to know is to look for Him. Where we find any of God's attributes, we will also find evidence of His presence. Godly love, the kind described in 1 Corinthians 13:4-8, is possible only because of the presence of God. The patience of God is possible only through His presence. The good that we see, the love that we experience, and the peace that surpasses understanding are all evidence of His presence. And we are drawn to God through His presence. Our flesh is not drawing us to God. The devil is certainly not drawing us to God. Anything that draws us toward God in the most challenging circumstances is possible only because of His presence.

So instead of looking for what we want God to do, let's look for evidence of who He is and what He is revealing to us through our failures.

As I reflect on the closure of Project Dream BIG, it truly felt like I was drowning. I felt my skills were not enough. I felt as if my own decisions were causing the issues that I was navigating.

But now that I look back at the situation, intentionally looking for God in it, I see His fingerprints everywhere.

The first place I see God in this failure is in how He drew me to Himself. When I was working on Project Dream BIG, I was focused on my abilities. It had not even crossed my mind that my skill set would not be enough, but as the organization closed, I found my attention shifting back to God. The fact that my own skills failed me made me painfully aware that my abilities are limited. It's interesting that God can use something like your own failure to remind you of how much you need Him. Sometimes I can find it easy to drift into pride, and I have noticed that God uses divinely placed moments of failure to reel me back to Him. Because the truth is that although this temporal world values success over everything else, God does not. Our relationship with God is more valuable to Him than thousands of grand accomplishments.

The second place I see God in this failure is in the evidence of His attributes. Throughout the Scriptures we see that God is faithful. God is faithful to draw people to Him. God is faithful even when I am not, and God was faithful even in this painful experience. God kept mentor–mentee relationships forged through Project Dream BIG. Although the organization did not make it to the level of success that I had anticipated, God was faithful to help mentors and mentees make and maintain positive relationships. God showed that with or without the organization, He was the One creating these connections, some of which will last a lifetime even though the organization did not. That was evidence of God's presence, His faithfulness in doing work that no organization could do.

I could go on and on about ways that I see God's attributes, promises, and mission in moments where I feel like I am drowning in failure. This is evidence of God's presence even in the moment that I have failed. In the world many people attempt to distance themselves from someone who is failing. We may want to associate only with winners, but God is present even when our greatest shortcomings are on full display. These moments of our lives are not hidden from Him. In fact God is near the whole time, drawing us to Himself, fulfilling promises and revealing His character.

Now it's your turn. Let's go back to that moment of failure and look for evidence of God's presence. We can look for Him in the situation, in the events surrounding the situation, in the people connected to you during that time, and in the path of your life after the situation.

Look for God's attributes. Look for evidence of God's fulfilled promises and for evidence of God's mission to draw us closer to Himself. Instead of searching for how we want Him to show up, let's search for who He is and how He has chosen to show up.

Here are some questions for you to ponder:

1. Where can I find the attributes of God (love, patience, mercy, justice, kindness, etc.) at work in this situation, in the events surrounding it, in the people connected to me during this time, and in the path of my life afterward?

2. Where can I find the promises of God at work in the situation, in the events surrounding it, in the people connected to me during this time, and in the path of my life afterward? (Consider promises God has made, whether they've been fulfilled yet or not.)
3. Where can I find the mission of God in the situation, in the events surrounding it, in the people connected to me during this time, and in the path of my life afterward? (Remember, God's mission is to draw us close to Him, to get rid of any lies or anything else that keep us distant from Him.)

Were you surprised by where you found God? Were you surprised to find how close God is even in your failures? As we intentionally look for God's attributes, promises, and mission in our lives, we find Him much closer than we thought. He's not far off, waiting for us to make our way to Him. God is in our situations, no matter how difficult they are. He is right there, being who He has always been throughout history.

The truth is that often we are not looking for God; we are looking for outcomes. When we shout, "God, where are You?" from the hospital bed, is it because we truly want God to sit with us or because we want to be healed of the ailment and we don't care how it happens?

When I shout, "God, where are You?" because my marriage is crumbling, is it because I am really seeking God's comfort and direction or because I want the outcome of my marriage fixed? We often miss the nearness of God because we were never actually looking for Him in the first place. We were looking for what He could do but not for His presence.

As we find God's presence near us in situations like our own failure, I hope we realize that if we truly seek *Him*—His attributes, His promises, His mission—we will find God nearer than we expected every time.

TRACING GOD

Scripture

> I am persuaded that neither death nor life, nor angels nor rulers, nor things present nor things to come, nor powers, nor height nor depth, nor any other created thing will be able to separate us from the love of God that is in Christ Jesus our Lord.
>
> **ROMANS 8:38-39, CSB**

Devotional

The apostle Paul wrote these words in a letter to the disciples of Jesus Christ in Rome. This is the same person who at one point was persecuting Christians and was confronted by Jesus Christ to change his ways. This is also the same Paul who had been shipwrecked, thrown in jail for something he didn't do, and abandoned by many of the same friends who had persecuted Christians with him. Disciples of Jesus Christ were scared of Paul because he was known as a persecutor of Christians, and the Pharisees didn't want anything to do with him because he no longer had the same beliefs as they did.

The same Paul who knew what it's like to fall short of God's expectations and to be in dark places wrote these words. He realized that no matter how far it may seem that Christ is from us because of our situation, God is never far. In fact, He is right here with us through Christ Jesus. If death is knocking on our door, God is there. If demonic powers and spiritual forces seem to be all around us, God is there. In our highs and lows, God is there. The situation may not work out the way we want it to, but God is there nonetheless.

As we explore areas of our lives where we may not have noticed God before, we discover that God was there all along. He is faithful to His promises to be with His people. God is never far; He is right there with us in our challenges. Let us be also convinced, as the apostle Paul was, that nothing can separate us from God, not even our own failures.

Reflection Questions

1. What did Paul mean when he wrote, "I am persuaded that [nothing] will be able to separate us from the love of God that is in Christ Jesus our Lord"?

2. Are you convinced of this? If so, what has caused you to be convinced? If not, what is holding you back from being convinced?

3. What are some ways you expect to see evidence of God's presence? What are some ways you have actually seen evidence of God's presence? Are there any discrepancies between your expectations and reality?

4. How has the journey we've been on in this book changed the way you view God's presence in your life?

Prayer

Dear Lord, let us truly and deeply accept that You are with us in hard places. You are with us even amid failure. Help us accept Your presence in places where our expectations of You make it challenging to see You. Help us lay down anything blinding us from seeing You in our very real—and often difficult—circumstances. Help us seek You in our hard. In Jesus' name, amen!

8

FINDING GOD IN THE STORM

Seeing Clearly When Life Is Out of Control

Have you ever attempted to drive in a bad storm? I have, and it was hard. I remember one storm where I had to pull over because I couldn't see anything. I wear glasses, and it is already difficult to see through glare from the sun in the day or from vehicle brake lights at night. Add in pounding rain that covers the windshield and you have a recipe for disaster.

The thing is, I never plan to drive in the rain. I have never looked at the forecast for a day with a high chance of rain and said, "I should drive on that day." The rain comes, and it is outside my control. Sure, meteorologists share forecasts on the news, but even though they base their predictions on patterns, they are wrong sometimes. The weather can be observed by humans, but we don't control it. What typically happens is that I start out driving in the sun and then an unexpected storm comes and affects what I'm able to see. The more familiar I am with a place, the easier it is for me to navigate it during a storm. Driving in a storm is much more challenging in a place I've never seen before.

We encounter storms like this in our lives. They may not involve raindrops that make it hard to see the lines on the road, but the storms of life can rain down circumstances and situations that make it hard to see God. Just as nature's storms are often unexpected, so are the overwhelming circumstances in our lives. There are times when storms come out of nowhere and make it hard to navigate life. I can guarantee that we've all been through one of these life storms.

We talked about detecting God when we've been abandoned, rejected, or otherwise hurt. We've talked about locating Him when we have fallen short. Let's talk about finding God when the circumstances of our lives are demanding and out of our control, making it hard to see straight, let alone see Him.

The pattern that we have followed is to first find yourself and then find God. In both chapter 6 and chapter 7 we described an experience and our resulting brokenness from it before we identified where God was in the event. This is a pattern we see in Scripture. During the Fall, God was not lost, nor were the first humans He had created. Yet He still asked Adam and Eve, "Where are you?" (Genesis 3:9). Why? Because they were hiding, intentionally trying to block God from discovering their mistakes. Notice God didn't force them to welcome Him into their vulnerability and shame; instead, He helped them see themselves and the situation accurately and then recognize God's presence in their personal storm. Although Adam and Eve responded to the question, they never invited God into the space of their sin. Instead they hid from accountability, attempting to paint the story in a way that allowed it to appear less incriminating. Adam and Eve left out details and became vague as they passed the buck to someone else (Adam to Eve, and Eve to the serpent).

Instead of doing that, I encourage you to be open about where you are now or where you were in the storm that we'll process together. The more honest we are in recounting our experiences, the easier it is to recognize God in the eye of the storm.

For this exercise, choose one moment to reflect on: a difficult one where everything felt uncomfortably out of your control. Where no matter what you did (or didn't do), nothing seemed to get better. We are going to use the reflection questions from chapters 6 and 7. And as I have said previously, try not to hold back. Be as descriptive as possible.

We are revisiting these painful moments because many of us have never processed them. No one teaches us how to process emotional and mental pain. Instead of processing, we push. We push past the tears, past the feelings, and we keep going. But when we push instead of process, where does the emotional pain go? *Nowhere!* It stays within us, seeping into parts of our lives where we didn't invite it, until it is processed.

Looking back at a painful moment with the understanding that pain will happen again is helpful. By examining the difficult experience, we can learn how we'd like to show up in the next one. And finding God within past painful moments will help us recognize God in the painful moments that we'll encounter in the future or the ones that we're in right now.

OUR PERSONAL STORMS

I'll start. As I've already mentioned, I have dealt with depression for a long season. I don't say this as a badge of honor but to give clarity to the reality that I live with most days. Depression feels very much like a storm that continues to swirl around me no matter how hard I try to escape it. After Hurricane Katrina hit New Orleans in 2005, I went to Louisiana to help with the rebuilding efforts. Debris was everywhere. People's homes were in shambles. Rescue workers picked up the pieces and rebuilt what we could. This is how depression feels to me most days: like a storm has swept through, and in moments of clarity I pick up the debris left behind.

I recall one time when I was preparing for a sermon and found myself sinking into depression. As I studied the biblical text, I slammed down my pen and began desperately using my strategies to feel functional. They didn't work. My mind swirled from past pain to future unknowns, and a dance between depression and anxiety began. Nothing I did made it stop. So I cried out to God: "Help me, help me, help me!" My cry started out reserved but eventually vibrated through my whole soul.

The help I was seeking did not come. I texted my husband to put him on suicide watch. I was so afraid of what I could do to myself at that moment. I crawled my way into bed, surrounded myself with blankets, and slept for over twelve hours.

It was a while before I began talking about depression in detail, before I recognized depression and anxiety as storms in my life. Personal storms often catch us off guard, and each one may require a different kind of support. Depression, for example, is a clinical condition that may call for medical intervention, while grief might require a more emotional or relational approach. Hurricanes and tornadoes both require preparation but demand different responses; the same is true for life's storms.

I have done a lot of work to prepare for my personal storms, much like the people in New Orleans prepared for Hurricane Katrina by boarding up their homes and evacuating the area. But no matter how much they prepared for the storm, it still left behind wreckage that was outside their control. Similarly, depression and anxiety can leave emotional wreckage. I began therapy to process my emotions and talk through the pain that seemed to lie dormant in my life. I explored medication options. I learned coping strategies. But there are still moments when depression and anxiety come swirling through and my best-laid strategies can't stop them. And after the storm has dissipated, I ask, *How did that make me feel?* It's easy to respond, *It made me feel depressed—duh* or *It made me feel anxious—hello*, but I had to learn how to sit with that question, to wrestle with the aftermath of the storm.

In moments like these I pull out the Feelings Wheel to help me express verbally what I am experiencing emotionally. I found that in that moment of sermon prep, I felt vulnerable.

The depression and anxiety swirl left loneliness, abandonment, and betrayal as I waited for the God I believe in to rescue me from circumstances that felt out of my control.

I did not ask for depression. No one asks for depression, anxiety, or any of the plethora of mental health conditions that exist. And although there are things I can do to prepare for flare-ups and to dissipate their impact, fully removing these conditions seems out of my control. And that makes me feel vulnerable and lonely. Many people don't understand what I'm going through, and I wonder why God doesn't still the storm and keep it from returning.

I honestly do not know if there is an area of my life that my journey with depression and anxiety does not affect. In the moment that I mentioned, my interior storm affected my energy level, my ability to complete a task that day, and my ability to show up fully for my family in the way I like to. Instead they were required to show up for me in a way I wish they did not have to.

Whew! The vulnerability of answering these questions is tough, but it is worth it. I promise I am not sharing my journey just so I can publish the pages of my journal. I truly believe that walking this journey with someone can show you that you're not alone. The storms in our lives are not the same; there may be some similarities but there are a lot of differences. But just knowing someone else has storms can remind you that you aren't alone. I pray that is what this experience has been for you.

Now it's your turn to share a moment that felt like a storm, where nothing went the way you expected, and there was nothing you could do about it despite your best efforts. Let's visit these steps one last time:

1. What is one moment where your life felt out of control?
2. Describe this moment in detail.
3. Evaluate how it made you feel.
4. Identify an area where you notice it affecting your life.

I think you know this by now, but I will say it again: Take your time. Don't rush through this section in an urgency to get through. It doesn't matter whether you read this book in seven days, seven months, or seven years. Do the work of processing events that you have gone through. You can do this reflection activity as many times as you would like for as many moments in your life as you would like. But I encourage you not to rush through multiple storms at a time. Instead, take your time with one until you feel you have processed it fully before jumping to the next.

GOD, WHERE ARE YOU?

After processing the storm in your life, it is time to jump into finding God. During my journey with depression and anxiety, I often cried out, "God, where are You?" but never intentionally looked for Him. I looked for the outcome and timeline I wanted, and when that outcome and timeline didn't happen, I was convinced that God didn't show up.

Now, instead of looking for our desired outcome or timing and calling that God, let us instead look for God! Let's look for His attributes, His promises, and His mission—and let's find Him.

We spend this search for God looking back at our past circumstances and answering three main questions. Those questions are as follows:

1. Where can I find the attributes of God (love, patience, mercy, justice, kindness, etc.) at work in this situation, in the events surrounding it, in the people connected to me during this time, and in the path of my life afterward?
2. Where can I find the promises of God at work in this situation, in the events surrounding it, in the people connected to me during this time, and in the path of my life afterward? (Consider promises God has made, whether they've been fulfilled yet or not.)
3. Where can I find the mission of God at work in this situation, in the events surrounding it, in the people connected to me during this time, and in the path of my life afterward? (Remember, God's mission is to draw us close to Him, to get rid of any lies or anything else that keeps us distant from Him.)

Before moving on, reflect on these questions as much as you can. Feel free to write down your responses or even work through them—and any reflection in this book—with a friend or therapist.

Take the space you need to find God in the storm. You might be surprised at where He shows up.

As I thought later about the storm I had navigated, I saw God in places I wouldn't have noticed if I weren't actively looking for Him. It's interesting that we can miss God's presence in the messy middle when we aren't actively seeking Him. But just because we miss seeing God doesn't mean He isn't there.

One of the clearest places that I noticed God when I began looking for Him was in His attribute of love. During my swirling storm, my husband, my best friend, and my children extended such love and patience that I know could only come from God. I can only imagine how difficult it must be to watch a loved one navigate depression and/or anxiety. You might become angry that your loved one is not fulfilling the position in your life that you think they should. Yet my husband, best friend, and children wrapped their loving arms around me, and I know the depth of their care and love could only come from God, who is Love (1 John 4:8, 16).

In John 16:33 Jesus tells His disciples, "In this world you will have trouble." It is easy to hold on to the promises of Scripture that seem pleasant and leave behind the things that are less desirable. But all God's promises are evidence of His faithfulness and sovereignty. This journey that I am walking through feels like trouble. But if the beginning of that verse is proving true in my circumstance, then the second part, where Jesus says, "Take heart! I have overcome the world," is also true.

We continue to revisit the truth that God is on a mission of reconciling humanity back to Himself. He is on a mission of relationship. I was feeling isolated in this situation, so it was challenging for me to see God drawing me close. But as I took a step back and viewed my mental health journey, I watched God draw me to Himself over and over. Amid the mental health challenges, God has allowed me to grapple with some unbiblical doctrine I had attached myself to that promised a perfect life if I did faith just right. This journey caused me to see God for who He is and where He was (not who I wanted Him to be or where I wanted Him to be) in my personal storm.

Finding God in the storm can be challenging. Much like physical storms, it can be hard to see due to consistently changing circumstances. That is why clinging to these strategies can be powerful. It is okay if we find ourselves engaging in these practices more deeply after a circumstance than while we are navigating the messy middle of it. All intentional reflection provides perspective.

The more often we engage in the practice of finding God in our most difficult moments, the easier it is to accept that even if we cannot see Him or feel Him right now, we have enough evidence in our lives and throughout Scripture to know that God is here. God is with us. No matter how scary the storm gets, God is with us.

TRACING GOD

Scripture

> I know the Lord is always with me.
> I will not be shaken, for he is right beside me.
>
> **PSALM 16:8,** NLT

Devotional

The interesting thing about this psalm that King David penned is that he did not say, "I will not be shaken because the Lord will work everything out the way I want Him to." He didn't say, "I will not be shaken because God does everything I ask." Or "I will not be shaken because God will immediately stop every storm I will ever go through."

David wrote that he would not be shaken because *he knows* that the Lord is right beside him. Throughout the Scriptures we meet people who learn that the true blessing is not that everything works out the way they want it to but that the Lord is with us. He is with us in the middle of our pain, disappointment, and frustration. When the storm rages or life seems out of control despite our best efforts, it can be easy to believe that we can find peace and hope only on the other side of this storm or dark season or time of feeling under water.

But the truth is that God often brings Himself into the circumstances of our lives and is willing to bring His love, peace, and strength into the very space we want to escape. He shows us that He is not afraid of the difficulties that arise in our lives and He is aware of the pain that we may feel as we navigate those hard moments. Instead of ripping us out of the painful places, He is with us and He gives us the strength to endure. He teaches us not to be bullied by our circumstances and reassures us that no matter what the world throws at us, He will be right here with us.

Reflection Questions

1. How does knowing God is always with you influence the way you look at your circumstances?
2. What are some of the hard things King David went through, and how do you think he recognized God near him through it all?
3. What is difficult for you to accept after recognizing that God is with you in your hardest moments?
4. How can you use what you know about finding God in hard places to recognize Him in your present circumstances?

Prayer

Father, thank You for being near. Thank You for not waiting on the other side of my storm, but for stepping right into the middle of it with me. When life feels overwhelming, help me remember that Your presence is my peace. When I feel like I'm drowning, remind me that You are holding me up. Help me trace Your hand even when I don't see the outcome I hoped for. Strengthen my faith, still my soul, and open my eyes to see that You are right beside me. I trust You, even here. In Jesus' name, amen.

Part 3
FINDING
US

Now that we have reviewed the importance of finding ourselves and finding God, it would be easy to end the book here. But we're not done yet! Let's be honest: After the Finding God section, you may have been left with a bit of tension. Yes, we are glad to see that God is with us in every dark situation and in every storm. But if God is with us, then why does He allow the bad to happen?

This question was the turning point in my life. When I leaned into seeking the answer for *God, where are You?* I never knew it would lead me to this truth: God wants to walk with us through life's ups and downs. God doesn't wipe out every painful moment because they are part of life. He could do so, but then we would miss valuable opportunities for growth. The goal of our faith walk is not to learn how to create a pain-free life but rather to learn how to live with God, be transformed by Him, and find ourselves in His love.

CHAPTER BREAKDOWN

Chapter 9 • What Is the Goal?: Moving from Revelation to Transformation. Have you ever wondered why God doesn't rescue you from every painful situation in your life? It's almost as if God has a different goal than we do. In this chapter we will talk about God's goal versus ours and how that affects the way He shows up in our lives.

Chapter 10 • The Power of Us: Discerning Our True Identity in God. We tend to look for God's power to show up in our situations, and oftentimes the first thing we get is God's presence with us instead. Is it possible that the true power is within our relationship with Him? Do we have the right understanding of the power that His presence provides?

Chapter 11 • It's Time to Grow Up: God's Plan Is Bigger Than Our Own. In relationships there comes a point where you grow up and realize that though the relationship is good for you, it's not all about you. There is a strength in the willingness to step into our roles as daughters, sisters, wives, and friends. Instead of being only recipients of love, we are raised to be bearers of it.

Chapter 12 • Allow Me to Reintroduce Myself: Living in Strength and Power. In the Western world we usually introduce ourselves by our accomplishments. When we feel like our lives are in shambles, introductions become difficult. In other parts of the world people introduce themselves by their family or tribe. You stand up not based on your own accomplishments but based on the accomplishments of the *we* you are part of.

GOALS OF THIS SECTION

In this section you will learn to

- understand the power within relationship;
- meet God's presence with your own;

- take responsibility for your part in the relationship; and
- walk in the power found in relationship with God.

I wrote this section multiple times. God had me erase everything I wrote because this is not about accepting the bad that has happened to us as all there is. God's presence in our lives and our relationship with Him is not the consolation prize after we don't get what we want. His presence is not the second-place trophy to His power. It took me a while to find hope in God's presence, and it might take you a while too. If you need to read this section more than once, that's okay!

9

WHAT IS THE GOAL?

Moving from Revelation to Transformation

When I got married, I was determined to have a marriage unlike my parents'. I was not going to argue. We were going to agree about everything, and I would have the most even temper possible. I had big goals and big plans for how I would show up in our relationship. Imagine my surprise when only a few months into my marriage, I was screaming at the top of my lungs about socks. I was losing my mind about these socks, but my husband was not matching my energy. He was visibly flustered by my lack of emotional control in the moment, but he wasn't losing his marbles with me.

Eventually he asked, "What is your goal here, Dominique?" For some reason that question was like gasoline to a fire building inside me, and I snapped back, "My goal is to prove I am right!" I still remember his response: "If you are proven right and our relationship falls apart because of how we are talking to each other, would that accomplish your goal?" Honestly, I had not considered the fragility of a relationship with another person. I had not considered how my mean-spirited screams would affect the person I was talking to. Did I really want to be right even if it meant destroying our relationship in the process?

During this heated interaction my husband and I seemed to have two separate goals. Mine was to prove I was right, and my husband's was to navigate this conflict together no matter who was right.

Our goals affected the way we showed up in conflict, the way we interacted with one another. My goal to be right allowed me to scream even if it meant his feelings would get hurt. His goal to be together caused him to be careful in his word choices so that he wouldn't divide us.

When I began my quest to find God in pain and suffering, I thought that once I found Him, He would fix my life. I wanted God to shield me from pain, to rescue me from it or even erase all the pain from my memory. My goal in finding Him was to never know pain again.

It was bewildering to realize that God has been with me through the ups and downs. He has seen the trauma, blocked me from some of it, and walked with me through the rest. Having God with me in the trauma was not what I had envisioned. I had believed that the pain was present only because God must not be. But after realizing that God has been present the entire time, it brought me to a new question: *What is the goal?* Or, more specifically, *What is God's goal?* It had become clear to me that God's goal and mine differed.

Over twenty times throughout the Old and New Testaments, God affirms His relationship with His people with some variation of "I will be their God, and they will be my people." He says this in 2 Corinthians 6:16, Revelation 21:3, Exodus 6:7, and Jeremiah 30:22, just to name a few places. Over and over we see this declaration from God that His goal is to be with His people, and for His people to be with Him. This means that in the hard times He would be their God and they would be His people. And in the easy times He would be with His people and His people would be with Him.

Throughout the Scriptures, the people God rescued, loved, and cared for did not have the same goal as He did. Often they wanted power, control, riches, or comfort. But God consistently did what was necessary to accomplish His goal, which was for the ultimate good of His people. He was with His people in the good times and bad. He was with them in the hard. He was their God despite their circumstances. But since their goals differed from God's, there was constant tension.

CLASHING GOALS

The goals of Adam and Eve, of Cain, of King Saul, the goals of the children of Israel, of Judas, the initial goals of Paul . . . all seemed to differ from the goals of God. God desired to dwell with Adam and Eve as their God and have them dwell with Him as His people. Their desire was for knowledge and power. God's goal for Cain was to dwell with him and to be his God; Cain's goal was to be better than his brother Abel and to be more liked. God's goal for King Saul was to dwell with him and to be his God; King Saul's goal was to be liked by the people he ruled.

Throughout Scripture we see a consistent goal from God and an ever-changing one from humanity. Humans grasp for more control and comfort, trying various soul-deadening means to meet these desires; however, whatever level of earthly control or comfort we attain is never enough, never satisfying. God consistently works toward the goal of dwelling with us. In the occasions throughout Scripture when humans choose to align themselves with God's goal, we see something amazing happen. For example, look at how Paul and Silas respond to being imprisoned for doing a miracle in Christ's name.

> After they had been severely flogged, they were thrown into prison, and the jailer was commanded to guard them carefully. When he received these orders, he put them in the inner cell and fastened their feet in the stocks.
>
> About midnight Paul and Silas were praying and singing hymns to God, and the other prisoners were listening to them. Suddenly there was such a violent earthquake that the foundations of the prison were shaken. At once all the prison doors flew open, and everyone's chains came loose. The jailer woke up, and when he saw the prison doors open, he drew his sword and was about to kill himself because he thought the prisoners had escaped. But Paul shouted, "Don't harm yourself! We are all here!"

> The jailer called for lights, rushed in and fell trembling before Paul and Silas. He then brought them out and asked, "Sirs, what must I do to be saved?"
>
> They replied, "Believe in the Lord Jesus, and you will be saved—you and your household."
>
> **ACTS 16:23-31**

Paul and Silas chose to dwell with God in a difficult time. Instead of racking their brains with anxiety, they sat with God and worshiped Him. The peace and power Paul and Silas needed were provided when they abided in God. And God's goodness and will were revealed to the jailer and his family as a result.

It seems that the goal is not to access God's power to escape life's discomforts. The goal is not even to escape pain (though that might seem alluring in the moment). The goal is to be *with* God—to be His people and to trust Him to be our God. It is not to use His presence to establish our comfort. Perhaps our disappointment in the times God didn't rescue us when we wanted Him to is because our goal was for Him to get rid of the pain. But God desires more for us than the absence of pain: He wants to use our circumstances—even and perhaps especially the hard parts—to show His love for us and others. No pain we can experience will outlive or outlast God's presence.

LAYING DOWN MY GOAL

When I made my middle school basketball team I had these grand plans of being the star player and reasoned that success on the court would lead to popularity off it. Of course, I never said these goals out loud, but they were in the back of my mind. As practices began, I learned that in order for the team to be successful I would have to lay down goals that were for my benefit only and adopt goals that were for the good of the team. On the court I had to be less focused on *me* than *we*.

Throughout this book we have been honest about the pain that we are navigating and have identified the realities of our present situation. We have also acknowledged that God has been ever present. His attributes and character permeate our lives, proving His presence even when we least expect it. These are opportunities for revelation. The next step is realizing that we are in relationship with God—He is with us and is beckoning us to be with Him. Intentionally being with God should move us from revelation to transformation.

Deciding to be with God leads us to become the *us* we were designed to be. Many of us in the West have been taught we should become the best *me* we can be with the best life we can create. What if instead we invest in living united with God? This will require us to lay down some of our expectations that serve us as individuals and instead pick up a perspective that serves the unity we desire to walk in with God.

Understanding where we are is a necessary revelation, as is understanding where God is. Accepting where we are *with God* and leaning into that togetherness is where transformation happens. When we recognize relationship as the goal, it becomes possible to walk through the hard moments. Even if His power doesn't remove the circumstance, the goal of being with God is still accomplished.

WHY DOES THE GOAL MATTER?

Where we set our sights affects how we live our lives and can cause us to have a stance of gratitude or resentment. And many times we set our sights on a destination we cannot yet see. It is part of the human journey: We can see a destination in our mind's eye before we see it in real life.

The goal we set our sights on can consume our attention. When our goal aligns with God's, it will lead to life and abiding in Him, which is for our good and God's glory. A goal that involves abiding in Him will allow us to find hope, life, and purpose in the most challenging of circumstances.

Understanding *God is with us* is a powerful revelation, but understanding *I can choose to be with Him* is true heart transformation. In each season of your life, you can consider yourself to be either far from the goal of comfort *or* safe and secure in the goal of abiding in God's love and presence.

If my main goal is to have a big house, then while I am living in a two-bedroom apartment I feel out of purpose and misaligned. But if my goal is to be with God deeply and always, then the time I spend in the cramped apartment may not be ideal but is still a blessed opportunity to be with God in the here and now. Shifting the destination we focus on changes the way we show up in our lives.

If my main goal is to be liked, and people lie to me and talk about me while I am growing a ministry, then I may feel unsuccessful. I may even be tempted to stop doing the ministry work I am called to. But if my goal is to abide in God, then I will focus on being with God amid any rejection by others. The rejection may still hurt, but I will be grateful for God's presence in the pain and see an opportunity for growth in the hurt.

WHY DID I GO THROUGH THE PAIN?

You may have read up to this point and feel a little dubious. Perhaps you're even shaking your head and thinking, *Are you saying I should just grin and bear the pain, that God is doing this to me because He wants a relationship with me? Who would want that kind of relationship?*

I understand your hesitation. We live in a fallen world, which means that sin is present. Even if we individually live perfectly without sin (which, of course, is impossible), our lives will still be affected by someone else's sin. Even if you didn't drink and drive, you could still be affected by a drunk driver. Even if you didn't steal, your life could still be affected by theft. For as long as we live in this fallen world, we will experience the impact of sin. Eventually God will replace this broken world with a new one (Revelation 21:1). But until such a time, we experience the effects of sin daily. Our trauma is a result of someone's sin. The trauma of others is a result of someone's sin. Someone else's trauma may have even been a result of our sin. So what is the solution? Will God put us in a bubble to protect us from every ounce of the world we live in?

Jesus informs us, "In this world you will have trouble" (John 16:33). In the current fallen state of the world, trouble is inevitable. But Jesus also encourages us: "Take heart! I have overcome the world" (John 16:33). He is with us. God never promised to void the world of trouble for us. Walking with the One who was victorious is the gift.

Jesus' prayer for us was not that we would be removed from this world but instead that we would be protected from the evil one even in the messy middle of it (John 17:15). The evil one has one goal: to separate us from God. Jesus was not asking that we be protected from discomfort or pain but that we be protected from the evil one's plots, that we abide in God amid the trouble of this world.

So am I saying that there will be tears; that even Jesus cried in this world? Am I saying that God is causing all this pain so you can have a relationship with Him? No. This pain was here before you were born. It is the very nature of a fallen world to be full of sorrow. I *am* saying that comfort here, in this world, cannot be the goal. A pain-free life in a fallen world is impossible. The goal is not to get everything you want from the material available here in this finite world. The goal is to abide in God, who loves you no matter the circumstances. In God's stability you will find peace, even among the instability of the world.

Shifting our focus to abiding in God will cause us to have to lay down some of the other things we were focused on. When we decide that it is *we* (God with me) and not just *me* that we are living for, it changes how we view our pain, our privilege, and our season.

This book is about recognizing where we are, identifying where God is, and deciding to live with God while navigating the hardships of this life. Finding Us is the section of this book that answers the question *So now what?* Finding

Yourself (part 1) is part of the process, Finding God (part 2) is part of the process, but Finding Us (part 3)—finding the new me that is only found in God as the destination—is the reason we are on this journey. The question we cried out at the beginning (*God, where are You?*) was what God used to get you here. He wants more for you than to simply find Him. When we abide in God and are willing to become *us* even in life's traumas, we can experience the kind of abundant life God offers us.

TRACING GOD

Scripture

> [Jesus said,] "I am the true vine, and my Father is the gardener. He cuts off every branch in me that bears no fruit, while every branch that does bear fruit he prunes so that it will be even more fruitful. You are already clean because of the word I have spoken to you. Remain in me, as I also remain in you. No branch can bear fruit by itself; it must remain in the vine. Neither can you bear fruit unless you remain in me.
>
> "I am the vine; you are the branches. If you remain in me and I in you, you will bear much fruit; apart from me you can do nothing."
>
> **JOHN 15:1-5**

Devotional

If a branch focuses on growing fruit, it has a poor focus. It could be removed from the vine yet not realize how detrimental that was because of concentrating its attention elsewhere. If a branch focuses on abiding in the vine, fruit will come in time. But no matter how much a branch pays attention to producing fruit, it will not do so without the vine.

The fruit of faith is a by-product of a life focused on the true goal: abiding in God. A productive Christian life and the fruit of faith can be generated in some of the most challenging circumstances. It can be produced when life is easy or when it's hard because the circumstances do not cause growth. Relationship with God is what reveals that even the most difficult circumstances have purpose and goodness in them.

The goal is abiding in Him.

The goal is life with Him.

The goal is peace in Him.

The goal is being a *we* with Him.

When we shift our goal to match that of the God of Scripture, we will see purpose in the most painful circumstance because we will see it through the beauty of the One we are designed to do life with.

Reflection Questions

1. What does it look like to embrace the identity of *us*—both you and God, together?
2. What does abiding in God look like?
3. How do we abide in God without spiritually bypassing the hard of this life?
4. What are some things that God has called you to lay down on your journey to walk as a *we* with Him?

Prayer

Dear Lord, help us abide in You. Help us focus on You and lay down any goals that keep our attention on ourselves separate from You. Help us find and embrace our new identity in You. In Jesus' name, amen.

10

THE POWER OF US

Discerning Our True Identity in God

My brother played college football, and he was good! I loved going to see him play. I didn't get to go often because I was in college in a different state. When I walked onto his campus I blended in with the crowd, and no one gave me a second glance. I joined the cheering in the stadium, and no one paid particular attention to me.

But after the game when I would walk up to my brother, the star player, he would hug me and acknowledge me as his sister. People who passed me by while I was in the stands were now determined to introduce themselves, and the girls who wanted my brother to notice them saw me as an opportunity to get close to him.

When I walked into the stadium I was not with my brother. No one knew who I was. But when people realized our relationship, my identity seemed to have more power, based on who I was connected to.

This is the power of *us* at work. So often in our walk with God we want to be recognized as individuals. We want to be recognized for our own power and control and independence. In many parts of Western society, independence is a sign of maturity, something that many of us clamor for. Yet our true power is in the identity we have *in God.*

IDENTITY THROUGH CIRCUMSTANCES

Oftentimes we attempt to find our identity through our circumstances. We introduce ourselves based on our circumstances with phrases such as "I am a teacher" or even "I am a successful banker" or "I am a starving artist." Each of these statements is an attempt to identify ourselves through the works of our own hands. The trouble with this is that sometimes our circumstances are not things we want people to identify us by. We don't want to be identified as the girl who was sexually abused even though that is a real circumstance we have been through. Or as a college grad who has a master's degree but no money.

Living in a culture that teaches us that our identity is based on circumstances can lead to a society of people hiding behind masks, unable to identify where they are or see where God is.

Identifying ourselves by our circumstances also causes us to identify God by our circumstances. We begin to look at our circumstances as the ultimate truth. For example, if I am struggling to pay my bills, I may be tempted to identify myself as a failure and God as not a provider. If I am chronically ill, I may be tempted to identify myself as a lost cause and God as not a healer. When we attempt to identify God and ourselves through the lens of our circumstances, we present a weak picture of who we are.

The true power we are looking for is found in our unity with Christ. When I got married, I took on my husband's last name. I like this tradition because it shows that who we attach ourselves to can impact our very identity. When I married my husband, our finances combined and our decision-making processes combined. He had access to my strengths, and I had access to his. We also learned each other's weaknesses, and we became known through one another. Often people who knew me and met him would identify him as "Dominique's husband" (and vice versa).

When we were looking to get credit, our application was stronger together. We became an *us*, and that *us* had an identity, gifts, and talents that were stronger because of being together.

This is the case with God. We want to see Him fixing everything that we want Him to fix (preferably in the way we want Him to fix it). But His power is best revealed in our lives in the *us*, in the unity. We started this book wondering where God is, and now we know He is with us. This can seem challenging, but God's presence with us places us in a position of strength.

The power and identity that we are looking for is not where we expect to find it. We think it is in having perfect circumstances, but truly it is in unity with God's Spirit. Many people around the world admire the American church because

American Christians seem to have good circumstances because of our faith. We can freely and publicly worship, we have access to multiple churches to attend, and many ministers throughout America are able to bring in finances from the ministries they lead. From the outside it looks like the American church has the power of God because of the relative ease of our circumstances. And then there's the underground church in China. Most of the believers who are part of that church have been thrown into prison for their faith. They have had their Bibles confiscated, and they worship God in hiding for safety.

But many American pastors who visit China are amazed by the devotion and passion these believers have for Jesus. In one of his sermons Pastor Wayne Cordeiro recalled the story of a woman in the underground church there. He said that as he read a long passage of Scripture, he noticed that she recited every word by memory. He asked her when she memorized all that, and she said, "In prison." Cordeiro asked, "Don't they confiscate the Bible?" She shared that people would bring strips of paper with the Scriptures on them. He then asked if they would take those, too. She said, "That's why we memorize it as fast as we can because even though they can take the paper away, they can't take what's hidden in your heart."[7]

Here is a church whose circumstances are filled with trials, but their posture is filled with power. This power is not from their circumstances, nor are their circumstances evidence of the power. The power comes from the believers' deep and intimate relationship with God. And the evidence of that power is how they persevere in challenges.

We are often looking for God's power to change our circumstances, but true evidence of God's power in our lives is the change that happens *within us*. When we abide in God, we no longer crumble at the first sign of adversity. When we abide in God, external circumstances can no longer bully us. When we allow ourselves to become an *us* with God and we willingly lay down our toxic independence, we may not find a pain-free life but we will notice power to stand securely whatever our circumstances.

Who is our biggest bully as humans? Many of us may say that it is the devil; however, the devil often uses circumstances to bully us. Many times our financial circumstances or our health circumstances seem to bully us, or our marriage or family circumstances. The devil uses these circumstances to get us to

- give up our identity,
- give up our faith, and
- give up our calling.

Much like a bully attempting to take a child's lunch money, the devil uses our circumstances to get us to give up much (while using the false promise that once we do, our lives will be much better).

A bully promises not to punch you if you give them what they want. But once you give in to a bully, they keep coming back, keep taking. The only power that the bully recognizes is when you stand up against them. When we abide in God, we get power to stand up against the bullying antics of the devil. We can boldly declare, "No matter what, I know who I am in God, and I will not give away my identity in Him, my faith in Him, or my calling in Him."

The power that we get through God's presence and our abiding in Him is the power to boldly stand amid hardship and suffering. We often think that the most impressive person in the room is the one with the most money or the biggest house. But the most remarkable person in the room is the one who is still standing no matter what circumstances are thrown their way. The power that comes from someone who walks through the hardest of circumstances *with* God is alluring. This is why the story of Paul and Silas worshiping in prison is fascinating, and why Joseph's increasing influence no matter how much others attempted to oppress him is so beautiful. When he was a slave, his master flourished. When he was in prison, the prison ran smoothly. God was with Joseph, and Joseph abided in Him. The same was true for Paul and Silas.

When you come into situations unified in Christ, you are bringing your new identity to circumstances that may be able to crush you but cannot crush the unity between you and God. When I came to this realization, I wanted to roll my eyes. I knew from experience that life still hurts when you are unified with Christ, that life can still be extremely hard. I am not trying to convince you that if you abide in Christ, life will become a walk in the park. But I am saying that there is a power to *hope* that is found only in unity with Christ. There is a power to *persevere* that is found in our relationship with Christ. There is a power to *stand up* in the hardest of storms because you know you are not standing alone. There is a power to *keep fighting* because you know that you are not fighting alone. There is a confidence to *keep going* because you realize that even if things do not work out the way you think they should, you can continue because your identity is found in the One who holds the future.

It's hard to bully someone who knows who they are and who has a relationship with God that is bigger than the giants of life.

But you have to let go of the *me* identity.

Over and over in this section I discuss letting go of the *me* and exchanging that identity for the *we*. This doesn't mean getting rid of all the things that make me unique. This means that now I am focused on the collective good in my relationship with God. When I enter a space with a *me* identity and focus, I do not take on my new identity as a unit with someone else. I think about this when it comes to marriage. Two things have truly changed my life and the very core of who I am: marriage and motherhood. Before entering the roles of wife and mother, I would walk into a space thinking only about myself.

I thought about my behavior from the perspective of what would serve me. I spent my money from a very *me* perspective, and I even went through hardships focused mainly on me and how those things would affect me. But when I got married, my perspective and focus changed. The way I introduced myself and the way I interacted with others changed. And there was such power in the unity of marriage that it altered how people interacted with me.

If a man approached me and asked my relationship status (even if my husband wasn't there) and I said, "I'm married," he would disengage. The way I interacted with the world and the way the world interacted with me shifted. The way I introduced myself and the impact of my introduction transformed.

When I became a mom another change happened. My physical makeup changed. I was able to nurse a baby, which I was never able to do before. I would wake up in the middle of the night at the slightest whine from my infant. I was the hardest person to wake up in the past, and now that has changed.

With both instances in my life, I changed. Becoming part of a unit deeply changed who I was and how I showed up in the world. A brand-new creation is formed within unity. Many things stayed the same when I got married. I still loved singing show tunes at the top of my lungs in the car, and I still loved dancing around in pajamas with my best friend. But other things were noticeably different. I was new!

The same thing happens when we lay down our independent identity and pick up our new identity in Christ. This new identity has a power and a resilience that is possible only in God's presence. Every struggle does not have to be fixed immediately because this new identity equips us with resilience and allows the difficulties of life to become testimonies that can lead someone else to freedom.

To find *us* we must first be willing to let go of *me*, trusting that in God we will not lose ourselves but rather more closely resemble who we were meant to be. In the early days of motherhood, I felt like I was losing myself. I would often cry out to God (and whoever would listen!) and say, "I am losing myself." This statement implied that who I was in the past was my true self, and this person I was becoming was foreign. I now often think of this process as a caterpillar-to-butterfly metamorphosis. Imagine you've crawled on your belly all your life. You begin to understand the dangers of your current situation and you begin to identify as a belly crawler. What would happen when you become a butterfly? It may feel very foreign and a direct affront to who you thought you were. But you haven't lost who you are because you have wings now. You are simply becoming more and more of who you were designed to be.

BUT THAT'S NOT WHAT I WAS LOOKING FOR

So you are almost forty thousand words into this book now, and you may be thinking, *This is not what I was looking for*. I get it; you may have wanted me to tell you the ten-step process to getting whatever you want from God. If I could crack that code, I know it would sell like hotcakes, but would we truly be any better off? Imagine that this book did teach you a ten-step process to getting whatever you want from God and that that process really worked. What would you want from God? What is it you feel He has not given you?

Perhaps it's to be debt free, maybe for your body to be completely healed, or for your loved one to be completely healed. And after that happens, then what? In this temporal world things will just break down again. Are you really looking for a ten-step process to make your circumstances perfect, only for them to break down again in a few months or years? Is that really what you are looking for? Because in this temporal world the perfect, put-together life will not last. So if that's not what you're looking for, what is?

Perhaps what you are looking for is not to feel tossed around in the wind, constantly fighting for your mental and emotional life every time something shakes you. Perhaps what you really desire is stability (and not the stability that comes from a job that is here today and gone tomorrow), or maybe what you are looking for is love, care, and belonging.

The truth is that everything you are looking for can be found in relationship with God. Miracles happening to our physical bodies or our material resources are awe-inspiring, but the true power of God is found in His presence. Because with God, our circumstances cannot bully our mood. And with God our stability is not rooted in the temporal nature of this life. In God we find everything we are looking for, even if our lives are not exactly how we want them to be.

Abraham Maslow, a twentieth-century American psychologist, was one of the founders of humanistic psychology. Maslow determined that humans have five types of needs which are organized hierarchically, meaning that if the foundational needs are unmet, it becomes increasingly difficult for someone to move to the next level until the first level is fulfilled. The order of needs, from foundational to aspirational, are

- physiological,
- safety,
- social (love and belonging),
- esteem, and
- self-actualization.

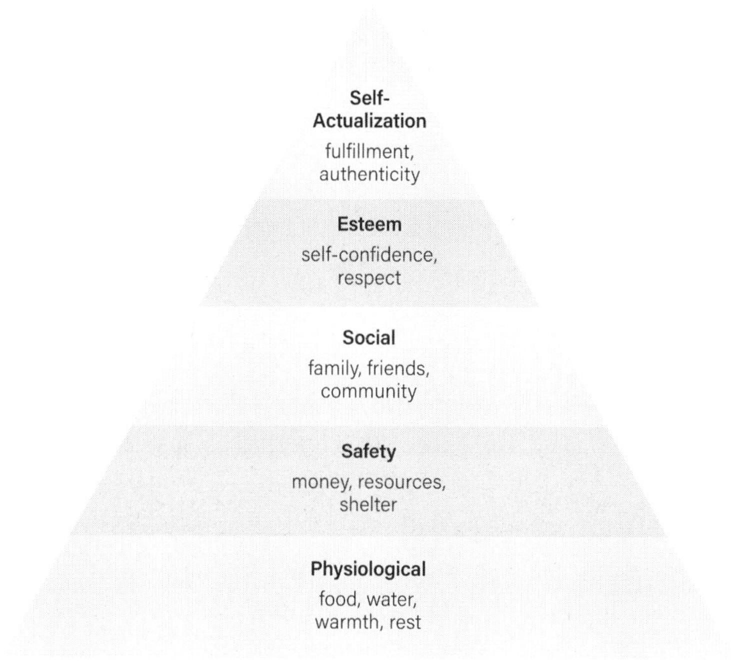

Self-Actualization
fulfillment, authenticity

Esteem
self-confidence, respect

Social
family, friends, community

Safety
money, resources, shelter

Physiological
food, water, warmth, rest

Often we attempt to fulfill these needs ourselves through our circumstances. But it doesn't work. Every human being has these needs, whether you are living in a penthouse in a prosperous city or in a shack surrounded by poverty. No matter where you live or what your circumstances are, we all have the same core needs.

It might seem cruel that people with vastly different circumstances come prewired with the same needs. Throughout the world you will find people with all different types of socioeconomic situations. And though we don't want to admit it, not everyone who is experiencing poverty will become a millionaire and not everyone in the middle class will become wealthy. So why would people with different external circumstances come prewired with the same core needs? Is it possible that our core needs are not fulfilled by our external circumstances alone?

If our core needs were fulfilled by external circumstances alone, those with more financial resources would automatically be happier and those with less access to resources would always be miserable. But that is not necessarily true.[8] We see in the early church that many believers experienced poverty. Some lost their material possessions to follow Jesus, and others lost their freedom; however, these early Christ followers were filled with hope and happiness even when their circumstances appeared dire (Paul and Silas in prison and Joseph in slavery, for example). How was this possible?

Because our power to live a fulfilling life is not found in the number or value of possessions we amass. Fulfillment is found in our relationship with Christ.

While fixing our temporal, earthly life may sound nice, it won't last. When we surrender our independent identity and embrace our identity in Christ, we can rise above our circumstances. Fulfillment is not found in *me*—it's in *us*. And as we live out of our identity in God, He gives us the ability to stand when it's hard, to worship through the tears, and to declare victory when everything around us looks like defeat. *That's* the power of us.

TRACING GOD

Scripture

> A mob quickly formed against Paul and Silas, and the city officials ordered them stripped and beaten with wooden rods. They were severely beaten, and then they were thrown into prison. The jailer was ordered to make sure they didn't escape. So the jailer put them into the inner dungeon and clamped their feet in the stocks.
>
> Around midnight Paul and Silas were praying and singing hymns to God, and the other prisoners were listening. Suddenly, there was a massive earthquake, and the prison was shaken to its foundations. All the doors immediately flew open, and the chains of every prisoner fell off! The jailer woke up to see the prison doors wide open. He assumed the prisoners had escaped, so he drew his sword to kill himself. But Paul shouted to him, "Stop! Don't kill yourself! We are all here!"
>
> The jailer called for lights and ran to the dungeon and fell down trembling before Paul and Silas. Then he brought them out and asked, "Sirs, what must I do to be saved?"
>
> They replied, "Believe in the Lord Jesus and you will be saved, along with everyone in your household."
>
> **ACTS 16:22-31, NLT**

Devotional

Paul and Silas did nothing to deserve prison. They set a woman free from the grip of a demon. You would think, after such a miraculous demonstration of God's power, that people would realize God was with Paul and Silas and that their circumstances would improve, but that was not the case.

In fact, their circumstances seem to get worse. One minute they are freely walking down the road, and a few minutes later they are beaten and thrown into prison. If Paul and Silas had sought stability from their circumstances, this experience would likely be extremely destabilizing. But instead something interesting happens: They begin to worship. Their song is not to get God to do something for them; rather, it is an opportunity to intentionally spend time with God even in prison.

Scripture doesn't say that Paul and Silas pray fervently to be released from prison or that they prophesy about their discharge. It just says that they begin to worship. The next thing you know, the doors of the prison fling open and everyone stays where they are. This miraculous sign is enough for the prison guard to come to know Jesus Christ.

Paul and Silas didn't have perfectly curated circumstances that gave them power. Nor was it the fact that everyone liked them, or that they had a lot of money (they didn't). On the contrary, their power came from their relationship with Jesus. And before that power showed up as open prison doors, it showed up in their ability to be grateful and trust God even when their circumstances were far from ideal.

Reflection Questions

1. What do you tend to focus on when you face difficult circumstances—your challenges or God's presence? How can you shift your focus toward Him?

2. Paul and Silas worshiped God while in prison, even though they didn't know what would happen. How can worship become part of your response to trials?

3. The prison guard's life was transformed because of Paul and Silas's faithfulness in hardship. How might your faithfulness influence the lives of those around you?

4. Think of a time when your circumstances felt overwhelming. Looking back, can you trace where God was at work in them? How does this encourage you to trust Him in your current situation?

Prayer

Heavenly Father, thank You for the example of Paul and Silas, who chose to worship You even in the darkest of situations. Help us trace Your presence in our lives, no matter what we are facing. Teach us to trust You not because of what You can do but because of who You are. Strengthen us to find our stability, hope, and joy in You alone. May our worship be a testimony to others of Your power and goodness, leading them to know You. Open our eyes to see You working, even when life is hard, and remind us that You are always near. In Jesus' name we pray, amen.

11

IT'S TIME TO GROW UP

God's Plan Is Bigger Than Our Own

I remember standing in my daughter's room one day as I was painting it pink. I used a roller and then had to go over the corners with a brush. I stood on a chair on my tippy-toes and felt a twinge in my shoulder blade as I reached as high as I could to paint the corner the same shade as the rest of the room. The next thing I knew, my eyes were filling with tears because I began thinking of my mom. Up until this point I had some resentment in my heart toward my mom. I thought she should have done things differently with me as a child. I also felt like she was closer to my brother. But in this moment, I recalled my mom painting my room pink when I was younger.

She probably had to reach high to get the corners, probably had a twinge of pain in her shoulder blades, but she continued. Why would she continue through the discomfort, when it was hard? That's when I realized that my mom continued for the same reason I was continuing: because she loved me. Her love may have looked different than I expected at times, but as memories began to flood my mind, I understood that her love was always present.

There comes a time when we must grow up. We recognize that our teenage perspective is not the most accurate perspective, and we begin to see the adults in our lives as individuals with dreams and difficulties, just like us. When we are younger we may think of our parents as heroes. As we get a bit older we may see all the things our parents didn't do for us. But when we grow up we begin to see them as people doing the best they could with the hand they'd been dealt.

Our parents struggled and did the best they could to survive this crazy life. We begin to see their decisions not as a personal attack on us but rather as their response to their circumstances, their attempt to navigate life's ups and downs. Part of growing up is being able to see life as bigger than yourself.

Instead of seeing my dad as just my dad, I began to see him as a Black man who grew up during integration, raised by parents who grew up during the height of Jim Crow. I began to consider how challenging it must have been for him to navigate these realities, along with the financial strain of being a young father, and how he showed up in the best way he knew how with the tools he'd been given.

Instead of seeing my mom as simply my mom, I began to see her as a Black woman whose dreams of running track in the Olympics were stripped away by a serious injury and who had to drastically shift her dreams. I began to consider the challenge of that dramatic shift, not to mention growing up as an only child navigating the divorce of her parents, the absence of her father, and the presence of her stepfather.

Growing up offers us a wider perspective. Life is not all about us. This awakening brings with it a wider capacity for compassion, love, and forgiveness.

As we grow up, our view of God also changes, from *someone who gives me everything I want* to *the ruler of the universe.* The One responsible for keeping the sun in the sky and ensuring that the earth tilts on its axis in such a way that its atmosphere can sustain life. As we grow, we also begin to see God as someone with a will that differs from ours, one that's for the benefit of all humanity. Because of this discrepancy, some of the things I think He should do may not be His priority. Or there may be a reason He didn't shield me from some of the things I wanted Him to.

As we grow up, we begin to notice God's plan is so much bigger than our own. And we see evidence of His forethought and faithfulness because as the days and months wear on, we see that even our pain has been given purpose.

THESE QUESTIONS CAUSE GROWTH

Asking deep, thoughtful questions is a sign of growth. As a baby we accept whatever we are given. As a young child we often don't even realize some of the difficulties we are walking through. Many young children who are experiencing poverty don't realize that this is not how everyone lives. Some young children experiencing abuse think that it's normal. But as you grow you begin noticing more, and one of the first signs of maturity is the willingness to ask questions and seek answers.

The cry that started this whole conversation—*God, where are You?*—is a sign that you are growing up in your faith. Your willingness to pick up this book is a sign that not only are you asking that question but also that you really desire the answer. And as we begin asking questions and God begins answering them, we may learn more than we ever imagined when we were asking. Often when we ask God a question, we expect a certain answer. The answer we receive may not be the one we expect, but it is the truth.

Asking *God, where are You?* led us first to answer *Where am I?* Uncovering the reality of where we are allows us to explore the truth about where God has been through our challenges. Both questions helped us realize that God is with us in life's ups and downs. However, that answer incited yet another question: *God, if You are with me, why did You let that happen?* And a part of growing up is a willingness to hear God's heart as it pertains to our most vulnerable moments and memories.

Growing up in the Spirit means accepting both that God has been with you your whole life and that although God may have made decisions you disagree with, He still loves you and wants the best for you. His primary focus is not always your comfort, but He is always working for your good. Growing up in the Spirit also involves realizing that God has the weight of the world on His shoulders. Much like painting my daughter's room brought me to understand that my mother had to mother me through her own pain, we must also recognize that God governs and makes decisions through

His own pain as well. As Jesus went to the Cross, it wasn't without pain and sorrow even though it was for our good. As God led the Israelites to the Promised Land, it wasn't without pain and sadness as they grumbled against Him and repeatedly chose other "gods" to replace Him.

Growing up is realizing that God is not just our God but the God of heaven and earth who has been constantly neglected and rejected by the very people He has created, loved, and cared for. So although He may not do what I want Him to all the time, God is doing an amazing job and is navigating His own heartbreak while working to bring about our ultimate good. Growing up is being able to still see God and His love even through our own disappointments. Yes, we must grapple with the tension that God's presence has not always brought about the type of rescue we were looking for. But eventually we comprehend that even in the moments that were hard, that we wish we would have never gone through, God was and is still such a good, kind, faithful God, who has not ceased to hold the entire world together.

As we begin seeking God, we begin seeing more of Him. We begin to see His pain and sadness and recognize that even amid it all He remains faithful and focused.

BUILDING A RELATIONSHIP OUTSIDE THE DEMANDS

A healthy parent-child relationship goes through many stages. The first stage is where the baby demands resources to survive and the parents respond. The baby is unable to see the parent as an individual; rather, the parent is an extension of themselves. Much like we might think, *This is my arm* or *This is my leg*, to a baby the parent is merely *my mom* or *my dad*. It is a difficult concept for a baby to grasp that the parent has an identity outside of them. As the child grows, their concepts of *mom* and *dad* grow with them. Eventually the child becomes a teen and begins to grapple with the fact that unlike their arm or their leg, their parents don't always do things the way they expect them to. The reality that their parents are individuals going through their own ups and downs has not yet set in; rather a teen might compare their parents to malfunctioning appendages, which can breed resentment.

But eventually, the child begins to see their parents as more than just theirs. Our parents' humanity becomes more and more apparent to us, and we begin to see our parents as more than just our servants. Our relationship with them begins to grow, and that shift even lends itself to us being able to care for our parents in their old age out of gratitude for their sacrifice in caring for us through their own trials.

Although God is not a human, our relationship with Him develops similarly. At the beginning of the relationship, we might view God as merely a means to gain the resources needed. We're grateful that we've found someone who can be the source of our joy, peace, provision, and eternal security. We look to God for protection and security and to meet our deep longing for love, which cannot be satisfied by this world. But there comes a time when we discern that the protection and love of God doesn't look the way we thought. A time when we cry out for God's protection and our heart ends up broken, or the loved one dies, or we experience trauma. In those moments it can feel like our view of God has shattered, and we wonder where God even is. This is a pivotal moment in our relationship. And much like the teenage stage in our relationship with our parents, this period of relational disappointment draws us to understand that God is not our servant, the One who does everything we want all the time. On the contrary, God is God, and even when He doesn't do what we want, what He is doing is for the good. And through the pain that we may cause God, He is making decisions for our good.

It is after that realization that the focus of our relationship with God becomes about more than just how God shows up for us—it's about how we show up for each other. We are grateful for how He has shown up in our lives and commit to showing up for God as friends.

Every relationship goes through stages of understanding and intimacy. Since you've made it to this part of the book, it seems that the question *God, where are You?* has led you into true relationship with God. One that knows His love is present in trials. It is a challenge to look at His presence with gratitude even if He doesn't show up how we want Him to, and to find that we can show up for God amid our own grief and pain.

TRACING GOD

Scripture

> The Scripture was fulfilled that says, "Abraham believed God, and it was counted to him as righteousness"—and he was called a friend of God.
>
> JAMES 2:23, ESV

Devotional

Abraham believed God even when his life didn't look the way he may have thought it should. Abraham believed God even when others may not have. Abraham believed that God was who He said He was and that God would do what He said He would do. This belief was bigger than what God would do for him in the moment—it was acceptance that God is who He said He is despite the disappointments of Abraham's individual circumstances. That perspective caused God to recognize Abraham as a friend.

A friend doesn't use you to improve their circumstances. A friend doesn't determine you're not present just because things aren't working out the way they want, or not see who you are because of the challenges they face. A friend sees you for who you are and the beauty you bring even in great sorrow. A friend sees your vision even before it comes to fruition. A friend appreciates your presence more than any power, resources, or influence you may have.

As we wrestle our way through difficult questions and life's disappointments and traumas with God, our relationship grows. A friendship is formed and deepened, the kind of friendship God longs to have with His people where we can see Him, appreciate Him, and affirm His existence and faithfulness even in the most difficult seasons of our lives.

Reflection Questions

1. What does it mean to you to believe in God even when your circumstances seem contrary to His

promises? How does Abraham's example inspire you to trust God more deeply?

2. In what ways have you experienced God's faithfulness despite facing disappointments or challenges? How has that shaped your relationship with Him?
3. How can you cultivate a friendship with God focused on appreciating His presence and character rather than just seeking His blessings?
4. Are there areas in your life where you struggle to see God's hand at work? How can you remind yourself of who God is, even in those moments of doubt?

Prayer

Heavenly Father, thank You for the example of Abraham, who trusted and believed in You despite the uncertainties and challenges he faced. Help me see You for who You are—a faithful, loving, and present God—even in my struggles and disappointments. Teach me to deepen my relationship with You, not just as my Savior and Provider but also as my Friend. May I learn to trust Your promises, cherish Your presence, and affirm Your faithfulness in every season of my life. Draw me closer to You and help me reflect Your love in all I do. In Jesus' name I pray, amen.

12

ALLOW ME TO REINTRODUCE MYSELF

Living in Strength and Power

We have made it to the last chapter of this book, and it has truly been an adventure. Together we have allowed the question *God, where are You?* to lead us on a journey of discovering where we are emotionally, mentally, and spiritually. That journey led us to uncover that God is present with us in all life's challenges . . . even when He doesn't show up the way we want Him to or think He should. And the discovery of God's ever-present nature led us to the question that hovers under this revelation: *God, if You are with me, why don't You stop this pain?* We recognized that God's goal is relationship with us—so if our goal is comfort, then that relationship is threatened.

Throughout Scripture we see that God's goal is to be our God and for us to be His people. And that this relational journey is often fraught with challenges. As Joseph experienced the fallout of rejection from his brothers and wrongful incarceration, it brought him to a place of closer intimacy with God. As Moses told Pharaoh, again and again, to release Israel from slavery, his relationship and trust in God grew until God spoke to him as a friend (Exodus 33:11). And the apostle Peter grew closer to Christ as he dealt with the reality of his own sin and grieved over the crucifixion of the One who changed his life.

The ups and downs of life change us, and if we lean into God and accept that He is with us even when it's hard, then the change that hardship produces in us is that of becoming a new creature. We are no longer a *me*, but rather an *us* with God.

I remember becoming a mom. I wrestled through nine months of grueling pregnancy for my first child. Many wrestle through months and even years of adoption paperwork and red tape. The process of becoming a mother is fraught with challenges, but in the end we are a new creature. We are no longer just an individual but are connected to—a collective with—this small person. Our identity is now associated with theirs. You cannot have that type of transformation without some sort of struggle.

As we look at the variety of stages of becoming in a person's life, we find that the deepest bonds and the most life-changing situations are typically forged in hardship. We transform amid difficulties. This transformation, however, requires more than passive endurance. It calls for active surrender—willingness to let go of the version of ourselves that clings to comfort and control and to embrace the version that God is shaping. Embracing who we are becoming in Him is not simply a side effect of hardship; it is the very purpose of it. The trials of life, though painful, serve as God's chisels, carving us into vessels that reflect His presence more fully.

Consider the refining process of gold. In its natural state, gold is often mixed with impurities, hidden within rock and earth. To reach its purest form, it must endure intense heat. Fire melts the gold, separating it from the impurities, allowing its brilliance to shine through.[9] In much the same way, the fires of our challenges do not destroy us; they refine us. They strip away the parts of us that rely on earthly security, leaving behind a heart more attuned to God's voice, a faith that can withstand storms, and a character that mirrors His love.

It's here, in this process of refinement, that we discover a profound truth: God is not distant in our pain; He is intimately present, working in us. He is in the moments when our strength gives way and we cry out for help. He is in the stillness after the tears, whispering that we are not alone. And He is in the transformation we see when we look back and realize we are not the same person we once were.

A friend shared a story about her journey through a season of deep grief. She had lost a loved one suddenly, and in the weeks and months that followed, she grappled with the raw question *Where is God in this?* She described how, in her darkest nights, she felt no miraculous answers, no immediate comfort—just silence. Yet, as the months turned to years, she began to see the subtle ways God had been at work in that season of grief. He had surrounded her with friends who showed up in small, meaningful ways. He had given her unexpected moments of peace, and He had slowly rebuilt her hope. Through the pain, she emerged stronger, her faith deepened, and her perspective forever changed. "I didn't just find God in my suffering," she said. "I found myself—who I truly am in Him."

This is the paradox of God's transformative work. The very situations we beg Him to remove are often the ones He uses to remake us. The places where we feel broken are the places where His grace rebuilds us. And the identity we cling to—our plans, our sense of control, our definition of success—must be surrendered so we can step into the identity He is calling us to.

When we embrace this transformation, we begin to understand that *God, where are You?* is not merely a question of proximity. It's an invitation. It's God saying, "I'm right here. I'm in you, working through you, drawing you closer to Me. Will you let Me show you who you're becoming?"

EMBRACING WHO WE ARE IN HIM

When we finally accept the new identity God has given us through our transformation, something remarkable happens. We begin to live with strength and power that aren't dependent on our circumstances. We no longer ride the waves of life's ups and downs, feeling strong when things go well and weak when they fall apart. Instead, we tap into a strength that is unshakable, a power rooted in who we are with God and not in what life hands us.

This is the secret to living victoriously, even amid hardship: embracing our identity in Christ. It's not about pretending the challenges don't exist or denying the pain that we feel.

It's about walking through those challenges and facing that pain with the confidence that God is with us and His strength is made perfect in our weakness (2 Corinthians 12:9).

The apostle Paul spoke of this kind of power when he wrote, "I can do all things through Christ who strengthens me" (Philippians 4:13, NKJV). Notice that he didn't say, "I can do all things because everything in my life is perfect." No, Paul wrote those words from a prison cell. His circumstances were dire, but his identity was secure. Paul understood that his strength came not from the absence of struggle but from the presence of Christ within him.

When we embrace this truth, it changes how we navigate life. We stop measuring our success or worth by what's happening around us, and we start anchoring ourselves in the unchanging reality of who God has made us to be. We become people who can face storms with peace, endure hardship with hope, and love others with a generosity that flows from the endless well of God's love for us.

Yet, this kind of power doesn't come from a surface-level connection to God. It requires a deep, abiding relationship with Him. It's cultivated in the moments when we choose to trust God even when we don't understand His plans. It's strengthened in the times we fall to our knees, admitting our need for God and asking Him to carry us through.

This is why it's so important to walk through life's challenges with God, not apart from Him. Trying to face life alone, even as a believer, leaves us vulnerable to discouragement, doubt, and despair. But when we choose to lean into God during hard times, we discover that He not only sustains us but transforms us in the process.

In this relationship, we find freedom. We're no longer held captive by the fear of what might happen because we know that no matter what comes, God is with us. We're no longer weighed down by shame or regret because we understand that our identity is defined by His grace rather than the past. And we're no longer powerless because the same Spirit who raised Christ from the dead lives in us (Romans 8:11).

This is the power of embracing who we are in Him. It's not a fleeting feeling or a temporary boost. It's an eternal, unshakable truth that carries us through every high and low of life. It is the power to live not just as survivors of life's challenges but as overcomers—people who reflect God's love, grace, and strength in everything we do.

So the invitation is clear: Walk through life with God. Let Him be your anchor, your guide, and your source of strength. Embrace the identity He has given you, and discover the power that comes from truly being His.

THE RELATIONSHIP THAT OUTLASTS IT ALL

What began as a cry of the heart—*God, where are You?*—became a deeper exploration of God's presence even in life's darkest moments. Along the way, we discovered that God doesn't abandon us when things are hard. He doesn't leave us to face the storms alone.

This revelation led us to the truth that shifts everything: Our comfort is not God's goal. His goal is relationship, for us to know Him deeply, walk with Him intimately, and be transformed into the people He created us to be. And the beauty of this truth is that this relationship can thrive—not just survive—through life's ups and downs.

We often think that the easy seasons of life are when our relationship with God flourishes. But our connection with Him transcends circumstances. It grows deeper in the trenches of hardship and shines brighter in the joys of hard-won victory. Life's challenges are not a threat to our relationship with God; they are the soil where it grows. When we choose to lean into Him during the storms, we discover a relationship that is unshakable.

Think about that for a moment: There is nothing life can throw at you that can undo what God has done in you. There is no loss so great, no failure so devastating, no storm so fierce that it can separate you from His love. Paul says it best:

> I am convinced that neither death nor life, neither angels nor demons, neither the present nor the future, nor any powers, neither height nor depth, nor anything else in all creation, will be able to separate us from the love of God that is in Christ Jesus our Lord.
>
> **ROMANS 8:38-39**

This is the foundation of our hope. This is the promise that allows us to walk through life with courage, knowing that our relationship with God is not fragile but eternal. It is not contingent on how well we handle life's challenges; it is grounded in His faithfulness, not ours.

And here's the powerful truth I want you to carry with you as you close this book: Your relationship with God will outlast any hardship you face. It will outlast the pain, the questions, the uncertainty, and even the moments when you feel like giving up. In Him, you are victorious—not because of your strength but because of His.

So when life's challenges come (and they will), remember this: The relationship is the goal. And it's a relationship that can thrive in every season. God is not just with you on the mountaintop; He's with you in the valley. He walks through fire with you, and He calms the storm (or calms your heart in the storm).

You don't need to wait for the pain to pass to experience God's presence. You don't need perfect circumstances to know His peace. Right here, right now, in whatever season you find yourself, God is with you. And as you trust Him, you'll find that His love, His grace, and His power are enough . . . to carry you through and to transform you along the way.

In God, you are more than a conqueror (Romans 8:37). In Him, you are deeply loved. And in Him, you have everything you need to thrive, no matter what comes your way. So go, walk confidently into life's uncertainties, knowing that you are never alone. Your relationship with God is not just the goal—it is the victory.

The question that brought you here was *God, where are You?* Often the challenges of life cause us to hopelessly cry out this question, but those same challenges inspire our journey for the hope-filled answer. God is here, with you in this situation, and your pain is a beautiful foundation for a thriving relationship with God (even if it doesn't feel that way right now). The ups and downs of life show us who we are in Christ. And now we can stand tall and reintroduce ourselves to ourselves, the world, and our circumstances as children of the Most High God. No matter what life throws at us, our identity remains, and the more we lean into it, the more our relational identity in Him grows. So even the enemy's best-laid plans will only strengthen our relationship with God amid the challenges.

TRACING GOD

Scripture

> We know that in all things God works for the good of those who love him, who have been called according to his purpose.
>
> **ROMANS 8:28**

Devotional

Life's challenges often feel overwhelming, like waves crashing over us, threatening to pull us under. In those moments, it's easy to wonder where God is and why He doesn't simply calm the storm. But Romans 8:28 reminds us that God is always at work, using every situation—no matter how painful or confusing—for our good and His glory. This doesn't mean that everything that happens to us is good, but it does mean that God, in His sovereignty, can bring purpose and beauty out of even the darkest seasons.

When we embrace our identity in Christ, we begin to see life differently. Instead of measuring our well-being by our circumstances, we root ourselves in the truth that God is unchanging. He is with us at every moment—walking through the fire, standing in the storm, and holding us steady when everything feels uncertain. This gives us the strength to endure life's hardships and even grow through them.

Our relationship with God is the one constant that will never fail. It is not fragile, nor is it threatened by the ups and downs of life. In fact, our relationship with Him often deepens in difficulty, as we learn to trust God more fully and lean on His promises.

Trusting God doesn't mean we won't experience pain, grief, or disappointment. But it means that we face those things with the assurance that we are not alone. God is with us, working all things together for good. The process may not make sense to us now, but we can trust that His plan is greater than what we can see in the moment, and His purpose is always redemptive.

As you reflect on this truth, consider how your relationship with God has been shaped by life's challenges. Have you allowed Him to draw you closer, to refine your heart, and to transform your perspective? Your relationship with God is not just the key to surviving hardship; it's the key to thriving in every season of life. In Him, you are more than a conqueror.

So today, take a step back from the chaos and remember this: Your relationship with God will outlast every trial, every sorrow, and every storm. It is the foundation upon which you can build a life of peace, hope, and purpose. Let this truth anchor your heart and give you the courage to face whatever lies ahead, knowing that in Him, you have everything you need.

Reflection Questions

1. How have you seen God bring good out of a difficult season in your life?
2. What steps can you take to deepen your relationship with God, regardless of your current circumstances?
3. What does it mean to you that God is present in both the good times and the hard times?
4. How can you remind yourself daily that your relationship with God is your greatest source of strength and hope?

Prayer

Father, thank You for Your unwavering presence in my life. Thank You for the promise that You work all things together for good, even when life feels hard. Help me trust You more deeply, especially in the seasons when I can't see the bigger picture. Teach me to lean into my relationship with You, finding my strength, hope, and purpose in Your love. Transform my heart through every challenge I face and remind me that I am never alone. You are my refuge, my strength, and my ever-present help. Thank You for the victory I have in You. Amen.

ACKNOWLEDGMENTS

Writing this book has been both a joy and a journey, and I could not have done it without the support of so many people.

First, I thank God, who gave me the words, the strength, and the endurance to finish this project. Every page reflects His faithfulness.

To my husband, Steve—thank you for believing in me, cheering me on through every late night, and carrying more than your share at home so I could write. You are my greatest encourager.

To my children—every day you inspire me to grow. Your joy, curiosity, and love remind me of the goodness of God in the simplest of ways.

To my family and friends—thank you for believing in me and encouraging me to keep going. Your love has carried me in ways you may not even realize.

To my mom—thank you for being my constant cheerleader. Your encouragement and faith in me gave me the confidence to keep writing when I felt like giving up.

To my dad—thank you for being willing to allow me to include a tough part of our journey and for having that hard conversation with me with so much love and compassion.

To my faith family—thank you for your prayers and encouragement and for reminding me of the importance of living out the words I've written here.

To my agent—thank you for seeing the potential in this message, guiding me through the publishing process, and being such a steady advocate for this work.

To my editor and publishing team—thank you for refining these words with such care and helping me share them with the world.

And finally, to you, the reader—thank you for opening these pages and allowing me to walk with you on this journey. My prayer is that what you find here draws you closer to Christ and strengthens your faith.

NOTES

1. Kylie Bolter, "Method Acting: What Is It and Why Can It Take Such a Toll on Actors | Other Performances Like Lady Gaga's," *Hollywood Insider*, March 1, 2022, https://www.hollywoodinsider.com/method-acting-lady-gaga-house-of-gucci; and Jennifer Bustance, "Is Method Acting Dangerous?" *Backstage*, updated August 18, 2023, https://www.backstage.com/magazine/article/is-method-acting-dangerous-76443.
2. For example, Benedict Cumberbatch. Christian Jarrett, "Acting Changes the Brain: It's How Actors Get Lost in a Role," *Aeon*, October 21, 2019, https://aeon.co/ideas/acting-changes-the-brain-its-how-actors-get-lost-in-a-role.
3. *Merriam-Webster Dictionary*, "cognitive dissonance," accessed May 2, 2025, https://www.merriam-webster.com/dictionary/cognitive%20dissonance.
4. While creating this Feelings Wheel, I referenced resources at "The Feelings Wheel: Unlock the Power of Your Emotions," Calm, August 29, 2023, https://blog.calm.com/blog/the-feelings-wheel and Julie Nguyen, "How to Use the Emotion Wheel to Better Understand Your Feelings," Mindbodygreen, May 23, 2021, https://www.mindbodygreen.com/articles/emotion-wheel.
5. Kyle Benson, "The Anger Iceberg," Gottman Institute, updated June 26, 2024, https://www.gottman.com/blog/the-anger-iceberg.
6. *Merriam-Webster Dictionary*, "failure," accessed May 20, 2025, https://www.merriam-webster.com/dictionary/failure.
7. Leah MarieAnn Klett, "Chinese Christians Memorize Bible in Prison: Gov't 'Can't Take What's Hidden in Your Heart,'" Christian Post, June 11, 2019, https://www.christianpost.com/news/chinese-christians-memorize-bible-prison-cant-take-whats-hidden-in-your-heart.html.

8. See, for example, Michele W. Berger, "Does More Money Correlate with Greater Happiness?" Penn Today, March 6, 2023, https://penntoday.upenn.edu/news/does-more-money-correlate-greater-happiness-Penn-Princeton-research.
9. Kristy M. Blyth et al., "Analysis of Gold Ores by Fire Assay," *Journal of Chemical Education* 81, no. 12 (2004): 1780–1784, https://doi.org/10.1021/ed081p1780.

NavPress is the book-publishing arm of The Navigators.

Since 1933, The Navigators has helped people around the world bring hope and purpose to others in college campuses, local churches, workplaces, neighborhoods, and hard-to-reach places all over the world, face-to-face and person-by-person in an approach we call Life-to-Life® discipleship. We have committed together to know Christ, make Him known, and help others do the same.®

Would you like to join this adventure of discipleship and disciplemaking?

- Take a Digital Discipleship Journey at **navigators.org/disciplemaking**.
- Get more discipleship and disciplemaking content at **thedisciplemaker.org**.
- Find your next book, Bible, or discipleship resource at **navpress.com**.

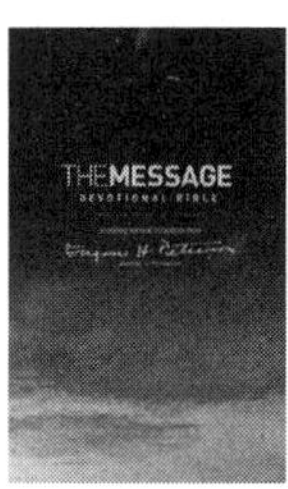

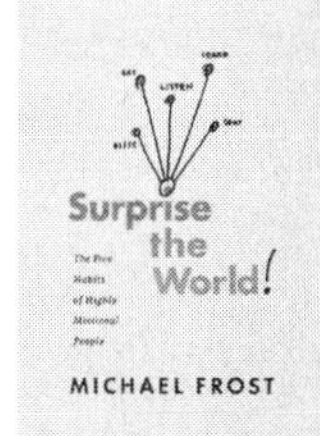

 @NavPressPublishing

 @NavPress

 @navpressbooks

CP1790